IT'S ALL ABOUT KINDNESS

IT'S ALL ABOUT KINDNESS
REMEMBERING
JUNE CALLWOOD

EDITED BY MARGARET MCBURNEY

Cormorant Books

Canada Council   Conseil des Arts
for the Arts   du Canada

ONTARIO ARTS COUNCIL
CONSEIL DES ARTS DE L'ONTARIO

Canadian   Patrimoine
Heritage   canadien   Canadä

The publisher gratefully acknowledges the support of the Canada Council for the
Arts and the Ontario Arts Council for its publishing program. We acknowledge the
financial support of the Government of Canada through the Canada Book Fund
(CBF) for our publishing activities, and the Government of Ontario through the
Ontario Media Development Corporation, an agency of the Ontario Ministry of
Culture, and the Ontario Book Publishing Tax Credit Program.

LIBRARY AND ARCHIVES CANADA CATALOGUING IN PUBLICATION

It's all about kindness : remembering June Callwood / Margaret McBurney (editor).

ISBN 978-1-897151-79-2

1. Callwood, June. 2. Human rights workers—Canada—Biography.
3. Journalists—Canada—Biography.
4. Authors, Canadian (English)—20th century—Biography.
I. McBurney, Margaret, 1931

HM671.187 2012   323.092   C2009-907184-3

Cover photograph: Courtesy of David Henderson
Cover design: Angel Guerra/Archetype
Interior text design: Tannice Goddard, Soul Oasis Networking
Printer: Marquis

Printed and bound in Canada.

RECYCLED
Paper made from
recycled material
FSC® C103567

This book is printed on 100% post-consumer waste recycled paper.

CORMORANT BOOKS INC.
390 Steelcase Road East, Markham, Ontario, L3R 1G2
www.cormorantbooks.com

CONTENTS

CAMPAIGN AGAINST CHILD POVERTY

JUNE'S FRIENDS

FOREWORD ᧿

AT THE TIME OF her death, in April 2007, June Callwood was one of Canada's most accomplished people — admired, determined, well-loved, and known far beyond Toronto, thanks to the many books she had written, her television appearances, her columns in *The Globe and Mail*, and her countless good works. But she was best known for her legendary kindness.

To say that she had lived a full life would be putting it mildly. This was never more evident than during her last three or four years when she faced her final illness with courage, clear-sightedness, and wit. Those of us who knew and loved her were not surprised.

By September 2003, June was unwell. In emails exchanged with two of her close friends, journalists Pat Capponi and Elizabeth Gray, she managed to tell briefly what was happening in her life — her cancer diagnosis, how she was dealing with it, and how much their friendship mattered to her. And she did it all with unfailing humour. As Pat put it, "June's emails were like flowering, personalized gifts she sent into the ether, with grace and love and undercurrents of farewell." Here are a few of them:

June to Pat:

September 28, 9:46 a.m.
We need to have a happy dinner together, but not for a couple of weeks. I seem to have picked up a bit of cancer and I am facing many tests to see where the hell it is. Eat your heart out!

September 28, 11:44 a.m.
I had my femoral hernia repaired a week ago at Shouldice. The surgeon removed the lymph node under it, and found it to be malignant. Now the search is on to find the primary cancer, which might be in the adjacent ovaries. I suspect that, but we'll see. Meanwhile the hernia incision looks ready to burst so something is going on there. Dying is fine with me, but all this foreplay is irritating. When I know where I am at, we'll celebrate.

October 6, 7:30 a.m.
Did I tell you they found another malignant lymph node? Near my pancreas. Cancer is like real estate — location, location, location. Saturday I had a mammogram, today a biopsy sample from my uterus, tomorrow a bone scan, and in

a few days a CAT scan. It's like looking for Weapons of Mass Destruction in Iraq.

This is a very interesting time of my life. Thanks for being there.

October 22, 1:03 p.m.

The colonoscopy and a gastroscopy were done Monday and were not too bad (lots of sedatives). Yesterday I met the oncologist and there will not be any treatment. She found another malignant lymph node, so that makes a total of four cancers, including the primary one which still can't be found. She's going to try to give me a timeline so I can make plans. Her idea is to do an ultrasound of one of the cancers now and then again in a month, and she'll be able to see how fast it is growing. Ingenious, eh? On we go.

What a rare and wonderful woman you are. I am one lucky person. Love you lots.

From June to Elizabeth:

October 23, 12:29 p.m.

I've thought of you many times, but I couldn't think how to start after hello. All this cancer stuff is only a month old. We are up to four cancers — counting the primary one, which is still invisible. The decision is to let things go. Too many cancers for radiation or surgery, and I'm too old for the massive chemo that might not even work. That's fine with me, particularly as cancers grow so slowly in the aged. The best part is that I feel perfectly well.

I'm in the getting-my-house-in-order stage. Grandchildren have been asked to please come and get their canoe paddles, summer camp pennants, and luggage with airline tags. The National Archives guy cleared out files yesterday, taking away twenty-four boxes of papers. He told me I'd get a tax receipt, which made me laugh.

All of this is rather satisfying. I often feel like a journalist. In the many many times I have been in waiting rooms with very sick people, I've done a lot of observing and there is a lot to observe.

I'm wiped from all the tests, but I'll get revved up with a few nights' sleep. My plan is to become a hostess, if I can remember how, and we hope you will come to see this astonishing sight.

From Elizabeth:

October 23, 4:52 p.m.
Mr. Gray and I accept with pleasure any invitation from you. But please don't be busy on Saturday, December 6. I have not sent out invites yet but that's when we will have our Christmas party.

From June:

I was thinking of a sit-down black-tie dinner for twelve that night myself, but luckily I hadn't sent out invitations so we are available.

From Elizabeth:

October 23, 4:00 p.m.
I don't know how you manage it … but you wind up making me laugh! From now on I will only write when I have something interesting or funny to tell you.

From June:

October 23, 5:20 p.m.
Please write anytime. There has not been a moment in your life that you didn't have something interesting/funny to say. I am off to Ottawa. I am on the advisory committee of the Law Commission, and I love those meetings …

ᢙ

THESE EMAILS ILLUSTRATE JUNE's kindness, her empathy for her friends' concerns, and her unfailing sense of humour; these were among her most endearing traits. They also exemplified her unique ability to recognize the importance of friendships and to treasure them.

If we hadn't known all this during June's lifetime, it certainly became abundantly clear in the days following her death. She hadn't wanted a big, public funeral — that wasn't her style

— so it fell to the people at Casey House Hospice and Jessie's Centre for Teenagers (now named the June Callwood Centre for Teenagers) to acknowledge the thousands of people from coast to coast who wanted to express their condolences. Phone calls, emails, and donations arrived in an unending stream at Casey House, as did visitors from within the city and beyond, to be met by hospice staff and by volunteers — those working for the hospice today, and those of us who had supported it throughout the nearly twenty years of its existence. Virtually everyone who came through the door had a story to tell about June, about what she had done for them, either directly or indirectly, and how much they admired her. They wanted to say thank you. Those of us who had always assumed we knew June well were continually astonished at the stories we heard: stories of her kindness and her generosity — stories that she had never bothered to mention.

It all came to a fitting end four days after her death. A candlelight procession of a thousand or more friends and admirers embarked on a two-and-a-half kilometre march from Jessie's Centre to Casey House, all to honour this woman they had loved and admired. Among the candle-bearers were June's two daughters and five grandchildren. Also on hand to pay their respects were other family members and several politicians — the premier of Ontario and the mayor of Toronto among them — along with countless friends and acquaintances.

Casey House has a tradition of placing a lighted candle in

the front window whenever someone dies in the hospice, or when someone dies who was particularly dear to Casey House. In keeping with that tradition, when the last visitor walked slowly out of the hospice that evening, the candle that had burned for June was extinguished.

DURING THESE EMOTIONAL, HEART-wrenching, difficult days, June's close friend, the physician Linda Rapson, told me that when June was admitted into palliative care at Princess Margaret Hospital, a few staff people asked, "What's all the fuss about? Who is June Callwood?" I found that hard to believe, having always assumed that most Canadians, even those who hadn't met June, had known who she was. When I mentioned this to my daughter, Megan, she said, "Mom, why not put some of the 'June stories' in writing so that she's not forgotten?" That query is what prompted this book. I hope it will tell us how, in all the good works she accomplished throughout her life, she was making a point: it was all about kindness.

But before we launch into these June stories, perhaps we should mention that June was not a saint, nor did she pretend to be. Everyone who loved her knew that. Her colleague, Gale Zoë Garnett, put it well, describing June as:

> a worker.... A journalist and activist who was determined to make things better in any way that she could. Having spent most of her life working with journalists and living with a sportswriter, she swore like a navvy when

exasperated — usually by graceless or misinformed behaviour. She believed in acts of kindness but did not suffer foolishness gladly; even when the fool was dear to her and she knew the dumbitude was temporary.... [But] June Callwood gave more, to more, more steadily than anyone I've ever known.... Alongside the ocean of giving that was June Callwood, we each periodically hold aloft our thimbleful of water.

Once you have read the following pages, I think you'll come to the same conclusion.

JUNE'S FAMILY

Family is what gets one through the night

— JUNE CALLWOOD

JILL FRAYNE ～

IN THE GREAT WEB of memories of my mother that surrounds me, one I remember for its delicacy is an encounter I had with her at the front door of our house when I was sixteen.

I had a steady boyfriend, the same one, all through high school — a fraught love affair that had me in thrall. I didn't join the swim team; I didn't go to slumber parties at my girl-friends'. I barely *had* girlfriends. My boyfriend and I stopped everyday after school where his road turned off and stood there 'til dinner time — and then talked on the phone after my homework until my father yelled up the stairs to go to bed.

My parents weren't happy about it. They recognized an obsession when they saw one, but they knew better than to try to shut it down. He was a nice boy, with good manners, loyal to me. I kept my grades up. Grounds for objection would have been tough to prove.

Two years along we started bitter, protracted fights, battles for autonomy, painful and consuming. I'd be weeping on the phone. My father would come and stand patiently in the doorway, waiting for me to pull myself together enough to say goodnight and hang up. He was providing ballast, though I didn't know what it was at the time. I felt a vague safety at the edges — that was all I knew.

One night when my boyfriend was visiting, we had a battle in my room — the first of a dozen breakups. It was an apocalypse. The rule was the bedroom door stays open, so my parents had to have heard us.

My mother was reading a newspaper in the living room when my boyfriend hurtled down the stairs and out the front door. After a minute I followed and stood wooden in the hall. My mother unwound from the sofa and came over to me.

"That's it," I wailed. "We broke up."

"Is that what you want?" she asked.

"No," I yowled.

She sighed. "Well, you had better go after him."

I did, and we repeated the rupture many times until we were worn out and could make it stick.

I believe this incident stays with me because I knew she didn't like him. Well, not him, but the spell we were under — the grip we had on each other. What she said in the hall came from a leap of empathy, and it was canny, too; she didn't advise me what was best, she gave me what I could use.

She had a knack for that.

Jill Frayne is June's daughter.

CATHY LEARD ⁊

THE FIRST TIME I met June, neither of us knew that soon we would be family. Four weeks later, her son Brant would be calling her to talk about our marriage. Naturally, her first question was "to whom?" Whatever private apprehensions she may have had did not deter her from insisting that she would be there and so she corralled Trent, tracked down Casey at the CNE, and arrived with something borrowed. This was a beautiful hankie that she herself had used at her own wedding. I never gave it back.

June's mother had a turn of phrase that I would say described June forever in my mind: she was a "classy dame." Given the nature of our second meeting we had a lot of room to get to know each other. While I was her daughter-in-law, we shared all the comedy and tragedy that families do but we also had a separate friendship through our shared life at Jessie's Centre for Teenagers.

I joined the task force that created that agency at June's

request and then joined the staff when we started the agency. For twenty-five years I have seldom looked at a baby without remembering June's belief that they are born as perfect beings and our role is to keep them as close to that as possible. Her own teen years were turbulent and I think her heart was always with these young women who walked through Jessie's doors. They are as brave and full of the possibility for greatness as June. Her idea of a perfect refuge from the disappointments or frustrations of a day was to rock a baby to sleep in her arms. When I look around the nursery at Jessie's I see that look on the face of parents, staff, and volunteers, rocking perfection all wrapped up in a tiny bundle.

Cathy Leard was June's daughter-in-law for almost twenty years. She worked first as a kindergarten teacher in Ottawa. When she moved to Toronto after her marriage to Brant, she worked in childcare and helped start a parent/child centre in the east end of Toronto. After two years on the Taskforce for Teenage Pregnancy as a volunteer, she began to work at Jessie's as a parent/child counsellor in 1982. In the past two years her primary role at Jessie's has involved training young parents in the Community Education Project to speak to youth and to professionals about pregnancy options, sexual health, decision-making, and parenting. They speak to more than one hundred high school classes every year. Cathy has married again and continues to live in Toronto's east end.

NELLIE'S HOSTEL FOR WOMEN

If any of you happens to see an injustice,
you are no longer a spectator, you are a participant.
And you have an obligation to do something.

— JUNE CALLWOOD

NANCY DODINGTON

JUNE CALLWOOD KNEW HOW to "press" and "impress." Perhaps it was her dauntless journalistic spirit and her passion for social justice, but it was hard to say "no" to June. Her unusual combination of driven determination and compassion meant that at one moment she could be seen storming the bastions of the rich and famous in search of financial support for her chosen organizations, and the next she was singing lullabies to the baby of a teenage parent or cracking jokes with residents at a hostel. She could work a room of potential donors with the tenacity of a general and the eloquence of a charismatic leader. Her guts and grace inspired many who willingly responded to her call to arms.

I recall one particular fundraising initiative for Nellie's Hostel for Women in the late 1970s. June had identified that the hostel needed to prove that it was meeting the needs of the women who utilized the service, and that demand was steadily increasing. Despite a lack of sophisticated computer technology at that time, June assembled a research committee, conscripted assistance from those knowledgeable in research design and analysis from the University of Toronto, and began the labour-intensive process of generating demarcated client cards. How well I recall those hilarious monthly meetings when June would breeze into the bleak basement meeting room and assist our team as we impaled client cards (with knitting needles!) denoting various demographic characteristics. In those days, data collection and analysis was labour-intensive and rather primitive. Nevertheless, she knew that the power of statistical evidence was essential in order to ensure that these services would continue. How ironic, I would later reflect, that June launched this campaign with knitting needles in hand. She was never averse to the idea of using every avenue possible to ensure that vital front-line organizations would continue to be funded and services would be available to those who so desperately needed them. Even a knitting needle — the quintessential icon of domesticity — might be transformed into an implement of subversion!

Like so many feminist reformers before her, June drew strength from her core experiences as a mother and grandmother and pushed the boundaries of complacency and inaction. She was in the trenches with us in the endless battles for the funding and acceptance of women's front-line services. With guts and grace she led the charge. She was the reason we went over the wall.

Nancy Dodington worked at Nellie's Hostel for Women from 1978 to 1982. She·then joined the staff at Jessie's Centre for Teenagers, where she worked for fourteen years, between 1982 and 1996. During that time, she coordinated the agency's relocation efforts to the Parliament Street location. Nancy now resides in Niagara.

DOROTHY RUSOFF

JUNE AND I WERE on the board of Nellie's Women's Hostel. One day in the early to mid eighties, we were having a meeting at Holy Trinity Church in a small room just off the back of Eaton Centre Square. A very inebriated, dishevelled man staggered into the room just as we were starting the meeting. Many of us looked at each other, feeling uncomfortable and wondering what we could do. How could we get rid of this man? June approached him. She gently guided him toward the door, with her arm over his shoulders, said some encouraging words. They must have been quite special, because he left, quite happily. We all just stood in amazement as we witnessed June's magic.

Dorothy Rusoff has worked in social service for twenty-five years in Winnipeg, Montreal, and Toronto. For the past ten years she has been teaching in Community Services at Centennial College. She has also volunteered for an east-end multi-service agency, a women's hostel, and a socio-legal clinic.

20

JESSIE'S CENTRE
FOR TEENAGERS

Jessie's gives babies a sound start by
helping their young mothers,
and what could be more important than that?

— JUNE CALLWOOD

KATE MANNING ✍

IT SOMETIMES SEEMS IT is only after a person is gone that we realize how much she meant to us. Luckily, I don't feel that way about June. While I learned a great deal about her life in the days following her death, I had always felt I was lucky to know someone as caring and compassionate as June Callwood. She inspired me from a young age — when I first met her I recall not. It seemed that she was always a part of our lives after she bonded with my mother, Linda Rapson, long ago. I didn't see June often but every time I did, she had a warm greeting and some sage words of wisdom. All in a matter of moments it seemed, since June was always on the run — off to save the world, or home to the wonderful man she called "my guy" or "Dreamy."

Because of June, I have been able to experience the wonder that is the June Callwood Centre for Women and Families (then known as Jessie's Centre for Teenagers. When I was in high school, I spent a summer volunteering in Jessie's nursery.

This was an eye-opening experience for a teenager who had never before seen a pregnant or parenting teen and who came from a privileged background. It was the most meaningful summer of my young life.

Years later, in 2001, when I was ready to volunteer in a different way, I turned to June for advice on finding an agency where I could join the board. The reply from June was instant and definitive: Jessie's was the perfect place and they needed board members. Since then I have therefore been privileged to be connected with Jessie's, first as a board member and then as a volunteer. More important, because of June, hundreds of children and their young parents have entered Jessie's doors and found a place where they can thrive. They receive top-tier counselling and access to resources, all of which are delivered in a respectful, nonjudgmental way by a dedicated staff.

I will also never forget June's visit after my twins, Andrew and Emma, were born. She came to my house in her Miata, breezed in with the most educationally appropriate (and non-gendered) gifts, and snuggled my baby while we chatted. At the time, I was pondering how I would ever return to work outside the house and leave these sweet babies in someone else's care. June very kindly and firmly told me that it was important for my personal well-being to go back to work and that I would be a better mother if I was intellectually fulfilled. Though I still struggle with the great juggling act seven years later, I know in my heart that, as usual, June was right.

Indeed, June was right about a lot of things. She was right

about fighting injustice and about passionately advocating for what she believed in. Because of her, places like Jessie's and Casey House exist, thrive, and do much good. June had so much of which to be proud but it was no surprise to me that at Jessie's 2006 AGM, June said that, other than her family, Jessie's is the thing she has done about which she is most proud.

I have a picture of June that hangs over my desk at home. I look at it often and wonder: what can I do next that would make June proud?

Kate Manning is a Toronto lawyer.

THERESA DOBKO ⋰

One

The power of one person
An extraordinary woman.
One Canadian
who has changed the social landscape of a nation
without election or appointment to power.
One of the greatest Canadians ever

Groundbreaking journalist
One of our first women pilots
Author of more than fifteen hundred news stories
or articles and thirty books
Television host and commentator
Founder or cofounder of fifty organizations or causes
Over a forty-year history of activism

If June had excelled in only one of these fields she would have been remarkable but she is beyond compare for the breadth of her talents and contributions.

June Callwood the journalist, pilot, author, activist, and national conscience had an intensely lovable presence, but her achievements were formidable. She was an archetype — no, an element, a force of nature, like water. I have seen her slowly envelop, comfort, and nurture and I have seen her carve a rapid's path through neglect, pain, and misery, even piercing stone, until she created a new landscape — one of righteousness and humanity.

Over a twenty-two-year period, and four organizations, June and I worked together on causes dear to our hearts: two AIDS organizations, one youth justice organization, and one centre for pregnant and parenting teens — Jessie's Centre for Teenagers, renamed the June Callwood Centre for Women and Families in 2007, with June's support. We became good friends and she even mentored me through a still-unfinished novel about life during the AIDS crisis. June's Centre would be our last working relationship, though it was one of the first groups she founded. June loved the Centre because it was grassroots, feminist, and supported the rights and dignity of the young women as well as the needs of their children. In the last year of her life, she and I worked to raise funds for the Centre to secure her legacy there. I loved each moment with her that year, though each moment was impressed with an undeniable sense of urgency and sadness.

What follows are some snippets about this great Canadian that will continue to inspire me for the rest of my life:

We are never too young to make a difference. June was forced to quit school at age sixteen to support the family and turned that crisis into a writing career.

We must fight to find our truest selves. June was a journalist and wartime correspondent when women were supposed to stay at home. When she was only twenty-two, she learned to fly planes when few women dared. She struggled with depression and with great loss but continued to write and to speak out.

Society must be pushed to change. June was a proud feminist. She was arrested in 1968, fighting for the rights of street youth to have safe housing and services. She helped found one of our first shelters for abused women, our first service for parenting teens, first AIDS hospice, pro-choice organizations, writers' groups, civil liberties associations, and others. June proudly marched in gay pride parades, long before most found it tolerable, acceptable, and FUN ... and she did have fun.

We are never too old to make a difference. At age sixty-seven June became a glider pilot. She flew well into her seventies. Her career of activism? She began this lengthy legacy in 1968, when she was forty-four, and continued until her death at age eighty-two. I started my activism in my twenties. Every time I think I might afford myself the luxury of finding "easier work" — now that I am fifty-two — I remind myself that I've only been at it for twenty-eight years and I've got thirteen to go before I match June's length of service.

All important change comes with a price, but the price is worth it. June was one of the first in Canada to learn that being a leader for social change means risking personal attack. She acted as a bridge between worlds: those powerful or not; rich or poor; black or white. In the early years, she often paid a terrible price, personally and professionally, from those in power and sometimes even from those seeking justice alongside her. How many of us appreciate the bridge as we travel over it, when all we know is that we are determined to get to the other side? June continued her activism until the end.

Anyone can confront injustice — and all of us must. June wasn't raised to be a leader. At a young age, she saw the pain of injustice and the healing impact of community involvement. She acted from those two memories. She asked us to embrace a moral code that transcends our differences. She defined kindness as the greatest moral virtue. Self-determination as a natural right. Compassion and care for others as essential to humanity as the air we breathe and the water we drink.

One person.
One person who became the river that carried us
along to national change.
We can live without everything else, for a time,
but we cannot live without water.
Who will be the water now?

*Theresa Dobko is a non-profit professional and community activist
living in Toronto. She misses working on all of those great causes
with June, the lunches over wine, and the talks of writing and
gardening. She misses seeing June drive away in her Mazda Miata,
with a little wave of her hand as she pulls away.*

CASEY HOUSE HOSPICE

The voices of Casey House are a hymn of hope.
They celebrate life and the human capacity to love.
— JUNE CALLWOOD

REBECCA BRAGG ⌁

ON THE MORNING OF Friday, March 23, 2007, in the inner sanctum of a small monastery in the foothills of the Himalayas, a group of more than thirty monks and lamas of the Tamang order of Tibetan Buddhism were praying that the soul of one June Callwood, born on June 2, 1924 and now dying half a world away, be granted a serene transition from this world of illusion into the next realm. Dressed in maroon robes, they sat cross-legged on mats on the floor in rows, pew-like benches in front of them. On these benches were long rectangular scroll scriptures from *The Tibetan Book of the Dead*, hand-lettered on delicate handmade paper. The air was fragrant with incense and the walls of the room covered with frescoes of Lord Buddha and various Bodhisattvas, people who have attained so high a level of spiritual mastery that they need not be reborn into this world of suffering yet have chosen to be anyway, reincarnating again and again in order to help all sentient beings along the road to ultimate enlightenment.

In Tibetan Buddhism, the greatest of all Bodhisattvas is Chenresig, the Bodhisattva of Compassion, who is believed to reincarnate over and over as the Dalai Lama.

Before the ceremony began, I and one of the monastery's senior lamas had lit, in June's name, 108 small brass butter lamps lined up on shelves in a small room downstairs. Symbolically, the light cast by these lamps was meant to illuminate the path along the way to her next birth, which would occur within thirty-nine days of her physical death. Tibetan Buddhism holds that dying can be a frightening and confusing experience for people but prayers for the guidance of the countless wise, powerful, but incorporeal beings who share the universe with us will not go unheeded.

Back in Canada, word that this ceremony was taking place had gone out through the June network so that anyone who wanted could increase the energy that would be emanating from this monastery in Darjeeling, India, by adding their own prayers for this woman who had given so much to so many and taken nothing in return, deflecting even praise.

AS I SAT IN a little alcove of the chapel trying to take pictures to email back to June via Linda Rapson, I suddenly found an element of humour worming its inappropriate way into my thoughts and feelings. Wondering what June, who swore allegiance to no organized religion yet was one of the most spiritual people I've ever known, would have thought of all this, I imagined her saying (although not entirely in these words), "As far as I'm concerned, it's all a pile of hooey, but thanks anyway."

"But June," I'd counter, "what if isn't all hooey? What if *they're* right and *you're* wrong?" Whereupon she'd laugh and say, "Well, it certainly wouldn't be the first time."

It seemed like — and was — years ago that the Casey House gang had its first farewell party for June in the home of Pearse Murray and Taras Shipowick. We didn't call it that, of course, but we all knew that she'd been diagnosed with inoperable cancer, had refused treatment apart from pain control and, when the time came, palliative care, and had been told by her doctors that she was not long for this world. That evening, I think most of us were a little startled when she walked in, as cheerful, radiant, and energetic as ever, to all appearances the very picture of robust health.

Sometime after that, word went out that since the kind of cancer June had was a glutton for estrogen, her age appeared to be working in her favour. She'd probably be among us for a lot longer than the initial grim prognosis had suggested — years, in fact. Was it not possible that she might not die of this cancer at all?

Maybe she'd meet her demise at the age of ninety-five after crashing her glider into the side of a barn. Or maybe "Saint June," who had worked so many miracles for others throughout her life, would be graced by a single one for herself. The cancer would vanish. No medical theory to explain this would be found. The ensuing publicity would bring representatives from the Vatican to investigate. And in her own cheery, charming way, she'd flip them the bird.

My direct association with June goes back more than twenty years but, indirectly, it goes back even farther than that, since she and my mother were both in the same high school class in Brantford. Like many of the people who worked so hard to turn her pipe dream of a hospice for people with AIDS into reality, I did not actually volunteer to head up the fundraising committee; I was conscripted by June in her trademark hit-and-run recruitment tactic, the success of which depended heavily upon her being out the door before her astonished victims had the chance to decline the dubious honour she had bestowed upon them. As she was well aware, saying "no" is easy. But *resigning*? That's much tougher.

I knew without any doubt that I couldn't do what she was asking of me. She knew without any doubt that I could. I was wrong. She was right. And I know that many other people who ended up giving their all to turn one of June's visions for a more compassionate world into bricks and mortar or legislative change have similar stories to tell.

I'm not a Buddhist. Like June, I belong to no faith group. God and I are not on speaking terms. But as I sat in the monastery listening to the hypnotic drone of chants and thinking of June, I looked up at Chenresig and remembered something else I'd read about Tibetan Buddhist belief: a highly evolved soul could be reborn into not just one but several bodies. And for a moment, the face of this serene image seemed to resolve itself into June's face and then, all too soon, she was gone.

For twelve years, Rebecca Bragg was a journalist with the Toronto Star. *She wrote this remembrance of June Callwood during the five years she lived in Darjeeling, but she is now back home free-lancing from Grand Bend, Ontario.*

HANK KATES

NO EVENT, NOR ANYONE'S woes, escaped June's personal concerns — she took the time to help, no matter how small the issue.

June did call me some ten years ago about the plight of a middle-aged lady who required support in dealing with her finances. This lady suffered from mental disorders and lived alone downtown in her house, supported by a small estate established by her late father and shared with a brother who lived out of town. She also suffered from a drug problem and could not manage her affairs. I assigned someone in my office to deal with this difficult situation, because she was spending money on her "habit" and not paying utilities. Long story short, we arranged to pay her utilities etc., and petitioned the trustee to advance more funds to accommodate her lifestyle, which included mothering a half dozen cats. Her brother objected, as he wished the estate to conserve its capital (I believe he stood to inherit the balance when his sister passed on). We prevailed,

June solved this lady's dilemma, and, of course there was no fanfare or accolades to be gained from this small gesture.

That was the June we loved.

Hank Kates was born Toronto in a lower economic scale household. He graduated Harbord Collegiate in 1957 and obtained a C.A. degree from Queen's University in 1963. He has enjoyed a career in public accounting, his clientele mainly in the entertainment industry, and has been an entrepreneur investor in various projects.

MICHAEL OSCARS ✑

THE FIRST TIME I encountered June was in 1986 when I co-chaired *Starring Act: A Celebration*, the very first AIDS fundraiser for what would eventually become Casey House through the auspices of the very new AIDS Committee of Toronto. June was our guest of honor, as was Lily Munro, Ontario's Minister of Culture at the time. I met June that night and remember how enthusiastically she thanked my co-chair, Donald Martin, and me for organizing the event. She fixed us both with what I came to know as "that look."

"That look" came at you mixing awe, gratitude, blessings, empathy, warmth, compassion, and absolute love. It affected you forever because "that look" made you feel that you had just done something or were about to do so — something so incredibly momentous that one of the very main reasons for your existence on the planet had just been defined.

June's great propensity was to bring out the best in you, especially when you had no idea that you had anything worthwhile within you to give, and "that look" only confirmed the obvious, if not to you, then certainly to her!

As the director of the first four DQ (*Drag Queen*) shows and as a former board member of Casey House, I had the privilege of seeing "that look" directed at me on more than one occasion. The one occasion however, that stands out more than all the others, is the one that I shared with the cast of DQ'92, the third of the four DQ shows I worked on.

First one needs to know that the DQ shows were a non-thematic pastiche of live comedy, glamour drag, lip-synching to big choreographed musical production numbers and where the words AIDS or HIV never crossed anyone's lips during the show. The productions consisted of forty to fifty-plus cast members, with nearly as many or more backstage production volunteers. Everyone involved knew why they were there and what they were supporting. The main objective was to raise as much money as possible for Casey House, make the audience have a good time and in doing so, hopefully have a good time in the process. DQ'92 was following in the footsteps of DQ'87 and DQ'87 — *The Sequin*. The first show, DQ'87, raised the crucial $38,000, as June was so fond of telling, that saved the day and allowed an eleventh hour purchase of the building at 9 Huntley Street where Casey House is located. Inspired by the completely unexpected success of the first DQ, DQ'88 — *The Sequin* raised $70,000.00 towards the purchase and installation of the elevator in Casey House. The dire need for funding of a home hospice program and the raising of consciousness of

Casey House's goals gave *DQ '92* its *raison d'être*, as did *DQ '95*.

The only acknowledgment of what the evening was in aid of would be at the curtain call when the cast would take their bows in especially designed Casey House T-shirts, lip-synching to an inspiring anthem to success called "We're Going to Make It After All" with a projection of the Casey House logo on the back curtain.

For *DQ '92* I decided to do something radically different for our closing number which was to have the entire cast sing LIVE! I asked a musical director, the late Allan Coffin, a wonderful man, to organize the entire cast into a choir and arrange a song ("Somewhere Out There," a popular hit at the time) for all the various voice levels. Allan was magnificent and worked like a Trojan, but no matter how many times we rehearsed the song it always seemed to fall apart. We were still slogging away on it a week before our first performance and though we were into complete run-throughs of the show, no matter how hard we tried it still would not come together. We had recorded a musical track for the cast to sing the song to and they either sang with it unevenly or too slowly making it sound very odd or like a dirge. I was despairing and running out of time.

June came at my invitation to watch one of our last rehearsals, though I had forgotten that I had asked her. I remember that this was going to be the rehearsal I was going to cut the song and reinstate our old closing number, but only after the run-through was over. I was depressed at the prospect, especially with June there. After introducing her to the cast, June said a few words thanking them all for their time and effort on behalf of Casey House. The cast were thrilled to see her and of course performed their hearts out for her.

Then we got to the closing number and I could see Allan's jaw tighten as he nervously stood in front of the cast to conduct them. I held my breath as the cast began the song and then I watched and listened in joyous amazement as they flawlessly built to its powerfully moving crescendo, all the while their eyes on June. As I was standing behind her, I quietly walked to the side of the room to watch her face radiating "that look." The cast were singing their hearts out, tears streaming down many of their faces looking straight back at her as they finished the song. The echo of the last note hung in the air for what seemed like an eternity with no other sound to be heard except mine as I heard myself say, my voice choked with emotion, "Ladies and gentlemen, thank you. We have a show." June began to applaud vigorously, joined by Allan and the rest of the rehearsal crew, at which point the cast broke out into cheers and applause and rushed from the stage to surround June.

From that point on the song worked and everything magically came together, but best of all I knew that it couldn't have happened if it hadn't been for June Callwood and "that look" of hers.

Michael Oscars created, produced and directed the first four DQ/ Casey House benefit fundraisers at the Bathurst Street Theatre, *which collectively raised $400,000.00. He served a three-year term as a director on the Casey House Hospice Board. He has, for over thirty years, been one of Canada's premier talent managers and is a partner in Oscars Abrams Zimel & Associates Inc.*

BILL CALKINS

WHAT I REMEMBER MORE than anything was the June rehearsal for the *DQ'05* show in the gym at Metropolitan United Church. That was the year that the committee decided to honour June and crown her queen of the queens. It was a Saturday — media day, confusion, and the June rehearsal. On that day, June's walk-on was worked into the show. She truly was a ham. One of the nicest things was that she addressed the former and current cast members by name — remembering all of their real and drag names — thanking them for their time and talent and for making a difference in the lives of the Casey House residents.

Rehearsal began and it was decided that June would be behind closed doors and, as the doors opened, she would appear — wearing a crown and a beautiful coronation robe. She would then proceed down the staircase to the front of the stage and then be presented with flowers, which I had the honour of doing. Everyone was in their place and, as we had rehearsed, June was coming down the steps, with someone holding the train of her robe behind her. She was greeted at each step by the hand of someone from the cast. Forty-five men and I managed to release no tears as this amazing woman made her way down those steps. She had touched our lives and founded with others an organization we loved. We all knew June was ill and we did not know if this would be the last show in which she would do a walk-on, but we all admired her and felt good knowing that we were part of something that was making a difference in the lives of others. June looked at us all as she made her way down to centre stage where, of course, she made a joke. We all laughed, but I think she was truly touched. On opening night we honoured her — and there was not a dry eye on the stage. June did tell the cast that, yes, we had touched her as much as she had touched us.

On April 14, 2007, it was announced at a *DQ* rehearsal that June had passed away and that there was a condolence book to sign at Casey House. Thirty-five men stopped rehearsing. They arrived at Casey House to write of how she had affected their lives and the lives of so many. They were the first group to come to the house and they were there because she had meant so much to them.

That is one of my June stories. She did make us laugh and, yes, she did have a foul joke to tell at certain stages — but this is my June story. She was real.

Bill Calkins first got involved with Casey House in 1992 during the DQ show. That was when he first met June and the Casey House family. "I was impressed with how the volunteers were valued and I was hooked." He continued to volunteer at Casey House, doing one shift a week, and also volunteered at many special events. In 1997 he joined the steering committee of DQ, and chaired DQ in 2004 and 2005. He is currently employed as the events coordinator for the Casey House Foundation.

SUSAN PORTNER

TO ATTEMPT TO WRITE a short story about June is to attempt the impossible. For those vignettes, the occasions, the circumstances, the times we have, each of us, experienced — whether the public naming of June Callwood Way, or the private moments when she was haunted and overcome with the grief of losing her beloved Casey — have played out time and time again.

Because when June was with you, for a few moments or for several hours, you were the most important, indeed the only person, in her universe at that time. I was so lucky to have lived the June Callwood experience through a long and varied tenure at Casey House and for four years on the board of Jessie's.

It bears recounting that, throughout the twelve years I was in the hospice, whenever June arrived at the house, the vibration was like an electrical current. "June's here": the words would travel to every corner of the house … and she never failed to stop and say hello, give a hug, spend a moment with a dying resident, pay attention to family members who were in various stages of grieving, ask how you were (and want to know the answer).

It is legend that the first *DQ* show in 1987 raised the necessary $38,000 to acquire the bricks and mortar that are 9 Huntley. In 2003 *DQ* returned to the stage after a six-year hiatus. June was part of that show, not just because of her cameo appearances every night, which were, of course, brilliant, but because she sat in a chair backstage for every performance and there are no words to describe how inspiring that was for the entire cast and crew. Just her presence. Just smiling and clapping. Just being June.

Volunteer Orientation. June's spot at nine o'clock Saturday morning. Coffee ready. Thirty brand-new volunteers at the edges of their seats. The coordinator (me) ready. I never failed to marvel at how this woman totally captivated an entire room of people for sixty minutes. Every. Single. Time. Over twenty sessions during my time alone (and there were many more, I know).

June wrote a book about Jim St. James — possibly one of the most poignant pieces of literature I've ever read. I was fortunate enough to be part of the volunteer team that cared for Jim during his hospice stay. To bear witness to June's bottomless well of compassion is to be moved beyond mere words.

No matter the gravity of the day/situation. No fear of impending death. No judgment of the harsh reality, nor lashing out of a person abjectly terrified at the prospect of dying of AIDS. Never rushed, always calm, genuine, free-flowing tears. The unique ability to commiserate with whomever, whenever, for whatever reason.

As sensitive and serene as June was in the presence of death, she was joyous and ebullient with new life. I witnessed this at Jessie's — another of June's creations — in the nursery where we would sit beside each other, rocking and cradling the tiniest little beings. The ultimate testament to the depth of her soul is that the babies never cried when they were nestled in her arms against her chest … she cooing gently.

In June's last email to me, she signed off by saying, "… that was a great lunch with you. You are a terrific broad. Much love, June." So June. Such a treasured friend. Such a terrific broad herself.

Susan Portner was at Casey House for fourteen years — on the Foundation board, as a support-care volunteer, coordinator of volunteers, and chair of DQ'03. She also served at Jessie's Centre for Teenagers for four years — as a board member and nurse/volunteer. She is presently the manager of the Financial Assistance Plan at POGO (Pediatric Oncology Group of Ontario), which helps with out-of-pocket expenses incurred by families whose children are in treatment for cancer. They and their families are as inspiring in their bravery as are the residents and their families at Casey House.

BILL WHITEHEAD AND "TIFF"

TIMOTHY ("TIFF") FINDLEY, LIKE many writers, occasionally had to do some rigorous self-editing on the way to completing a novel. With *Famous Last Words*, his story about the role of the Duke and Duchess of Windsor in the rise of fascism in the 1930s, he realized he had to cut a whole storyline in order to keep the work at a manageable length. The passage centred on a woman named Jane Porter, one of whose children had given her a toy sheriff's badge to wear.

Years later, in his first autobiographical work, *Inside Memory*, he published what had been deleted from *Famous Last Words*, along with the following introduction, which he had written in 1987 as part of the program notes for a Tribute to June Callwood — one of the fundraising events that preceded the opening of Toronto's AIDS hospice, Casey House, which had been initiated and developed by June.

THERE WAS A PARADOX in June Callwood of which nearly everyone who worked with her was aware. She had a way of turning up for riot duty looking like a million dollars. One day — I can't remember what it was we were doing, but it certainly wasn't the cocktail circuit — June turned up in one of her super-elegant outfits with a star attached to her lapel. Not just any star, mind you. It was made of tin — and I think it came from a box of Cheerios.

"I see you're looking at my star," she said.

"That's right," I said. "It's … interesting, to say the least."

"My daughter gave it to me," she said. And she leaned forward, showing it off. "See what it says?"

I look more closely. Then I blinked — and sat back, chastened. Someone, at last, had done her justice.

Written on the star was a single word:

SHERIFF.

If only it were true.

Timothy Findley was the life partner of Bill Whitehead. Both were volunteers at Casey House during its formative years.

SALLY SIMPSON

ONE DAY BACK IN the mid 1980s, June Callwood had an idea. She envisioned a safe, caring, comfortable place for people who were living with HIV/AIDS — a place to live, and to die. She saw a staff of committed, loving people who were dedicated to gaining expertise in the field of HIV/AIDS in whom these residents could entrust their lives, and their deaths. With dogged determination, through the years, the days, through the eleventh hour and beyond, June fought to see this dream come to fruition. On March 1, 1988, Casey House opened its doors. It was the first AIDS hospice in Canada. Since that time, Casey House has served thousands of people living with HIV/AIDS and their loved ones. June played a pivotal role in shaping the creation of that wonderful organization.

I believe that the fruition of June's dream, the establishment of Casey House, helped to shape the face of HIV/AIDS across Canada.

June's own philosophy of compassion and tenderness is still

reflected in the work done by the staff at Casey House. Her vision for people with HIV/AIDS impacted each of us, whether we knew her personally or from a distance.

Socrates once said, "Let him who would move the world first move himself." June showed us what we each of us can do, what each of us can be, in serving others. She had the wonderful ability to draw people together, those who are of like minds and hearts, and lead them to conquer just about anything.

I was fortunate to know June during the thirteen years that I proudly called Casey House my workplace. I saw her face seemingly insurmountable challenges, both political and personal, in her quest to right the injustices with which so many people live.

Once upon a time, I told June that I wanted to grow up to be her. Well, the years have passed (see the grey hairs sprouting?) and I am still not her. But I do strive to care and love in the spirit that June would have. June was a model for all of us.

Sally Simpson is a nurse practitioner who has worked exclusively in the field of HIV/AIDS for the last eighteen years. A member of the board of the Canadian Association of Nurses in AIDS Care, she is currently a student in the Master of Nursing/Acute Care Nurse Practitioner program at the University of Toronto.

DEVON STUTT ∽

I FIRST CAME TO really know June at the start of Casey House. We were a small group who wanted to create an AIDS Hospice; we hadn't even thought of the name Casey House — that was a year away. June she would continue to write on her typewriter, but wanted to save her work on a computer. (It took a year to get rid of that typewriter.) I was delighted when she asked me to recommend a computer — one that could hold all her work.

Months of hospice meetings came and went. June got a computer and I was invited to drop by for Sunday brunch to see it — an Avro, which I had been using at the Toronto General Hospital. She was pleased to learn that the guy who started that computer company was part of the Avro Arrow project — the ill-fated Malton-based program that developed a sleek white jet interceptor — and this was special to June. So I was now her official computer guy ... for me, better than the royal seal.

In those pre-Windows days of DOS, there were many issues that June needed help with, such as how to save her work on floppy discs (remember those five-inch diskettes?) and why a C drive was her hard drive, but she should save her work on the A drive. ("What's wrong with the C drive?") We had many short talks and I just left instructions.

Now, this was something that June wasn't used to. June helped people, not the other way around. I got to see that some of her strength was in her independence, which was tied to her sense of not needing and, even more importantly, not wanting help herself.

June started to give me bottles of champagne. Every time I was there. Now, I could manage with a bottle or two every few months, but not one every other week. I didn't want June to pay me — helping her was my reward. So I started making excuses for not being able to help her when she was at home. And I very politely asked her to stop giving me champagne, but she wouldn't hear of it. "Who wouldn't want champagne?"

I began dropping by her house in the middle of the day, when I knew she would be out. Knowing that she never locked her doors, I parked right in front of the house, making it very clear to the neighbours that I was going into June's home. I walked slowly up the drive to the side door. If I saw a neighbour, I waved and shouted "Hello!" I wanted to explain to them that I was a friend of June's and not a burglar.

Sometimes June came home to find me at her computer. After a big hug — the world's best — off she'd go to the cellar for another bottle of champagne. When she told me she had become a Lay Bencher for the Law Society of Upper Canada and was helping to select champagne for their cellar, I almost fell over. Would there be no end to the champagne? By this time, I was in a small one-bedroom flat and both the hall and bedroom closets were full of champagne. What would my boyfriend think? (Let's just not go there … okay?) I had to find a graceful way to stop helping June.

I found a computer consultant who was an Avro technical specialist and after just one conversation I knew he and June would be friends. They worked well together for years, and I'm told she paid him in dollars. I still have a few bottles of June's champagne left, but keep them for very special friends.

Devon Stutt was an IT specialist who played senior consulting roles at Toronto Hospital, the Canadian Securities Institute, and, at his death, was manager of Information Systems at the Ontario College of Teachers. He also served on the boards of Casey House Hospice and Fife House, which provides secure, affordable supportive housing and services to people living with HIV/AIDS. Devon died on January 20, 2008.

JIM BRATTON

THERE ISN'T JUST ONE story about June. There are six years of stories, woven together with emerging themes: passion, compassion, tenacity, respect, inspiration. Tireless advocate. Great sense of humour. Fabulous legs. A wonderful teacher who generously shared her many gifts.

"Hi sweetie," she chirped as she struggled up the stairs to my office. "How are you doing?" "How are your kids?" "How's Drew?" "How's Casey House?" I felt special. I watched her in conversation with others: totally focused, gently caressing a hand, smiling, nodding her head. She had the knack.

No matter what your station in life, when June Callwood was talking with you, she made you feel you were the most important person in her life; and, at that moment, you were.

"Jim, June here. I can't talk long. I may not be at tomorrow's meeting. I'm in Ottawa at a protest. I may be in jail." In 2004, Margaret McBurney, Chris Kelly, Sandy Houston, David Currah, and I gathered at the home of Heather Conway and Camilla Gibb. June was not well, and we wanted to do something lasting to honour her. Heather said that June's legacy went far beyond Casey House and we agreed that her lifelong commitment to social justice should be our focus. June was arguably Canada's best-known social activist and had founded more than fifty social action organizations. We weren't sure how our ideas would become reality. Days later, Marnie Kinsley had the answer: "Victoria University at the University of Toronto has a program in social justice. A perfect fit!" Within weeks, we met with Vic's president Paul Gooch and Martha Drake from Vic's advancement team. The June Callwood Professorship in Social Justice was born.

Marilyn J. Legge, June Callwood Professor in Social Justice, said, "Throughout her life June Callwood sent out sparks to ignite the hearts and minds and action for social justice. In the Vic One course, students help to carry on her legacy: to recognize injustice and to do something about it."

WHEN I FIRST MET June, I asked her how often she would be available to help the Casey House Foundation. Her response was, "Ask me for everything; if I can't, I'll tell you." Rarely did she say no. On rare occasions, she said she was not feeling well.

June came to every event (and we had many) and gave tours to more donors than I can count — to Miss Universe, to Stephen Lewis, to the famous and the not so famous. She regularly came to Casey House to offer support, encouragement, and her dazzling smile to the residents and staff members.

June Callwood was one of the most unselfish people I have met.

Was June amazing? Yes. Perfect? No. Yet those individuals who did not necessarily like her style respected her accomplishments. In terms of her commitment to making Canada and this world a better place, she was about as perfect as you can get.

June Callwood may not be with us physically, but she will always be in our hearts and, hopefully, our actions.

Jim Bratton was Executive Director, Casey House Foundation, 2001–2005. He is an American-Canadian and lives in Niagara-on-the-Lake with his British-Canadian partner of twenty-one years, Drew Tait. He is a devoted father, and grandfather and a Member of the June Callwood Fan Club.

NIK MANOJLOVICH

Humble June

I used to host "Lunch with June" during my tenure as chair of the board. It was a great opportunity to greet and thank donors, and June always attended to share the story of how Casey House came into being. At the end of each, I'd give June a hug and thank her profusely for her time and effort. She'd smile politely and make light of her efforts. "I didn't do anything except show up to eat, and you guys are doing all the hard work!" Her humility somehow inspired me to work harder and with more purpose. It was like a silent agreement. "We're both doing what we can, the best way that we can." Funny, we coordinated the luncheons and June served up humble pie, each and every time.

Stoic June

I remember learning of June's illness early on and I offered to have a video produced of her touring Casey House. She agreed without hesitation and appeared on the day of the shoot, smartly dressed. It amazed me how she smiled through it all while many of us struggled to hold back tears. Here was our founder allowing us to document her tour of the hospice, knowing full well that we'd need this echo of her presence long after she'd gone. She maintained her quick wit and flawless sense of timing. I checked in right at the beginning: "June, you okay?" Quick as a whip, she replied, "Yes Mr. de Mille, I'm ready for my close-up," and then snapped her head left and right, saying, "Which side do you think has less wrinkles?" She was all about getting over whatever bugged her.

June the Author

I did an introduction at the fifteenth anniversary of Casey House and actually ripped the lyrics for "Bridge over Troubled Water" from a copy of June's book *Twelve Weeks in Spring*. I read the lyrics to the room that evening, thanked everyone for their contributions, left the stage, and took my seat. Thankfully, I remembered to have everyone seated at my table that evening sign the page I had torn from the book. The next morning, I took the page from my tuxedo and was surprised to see something above June's signature. She had written, "Put It Back!" I called her the following day to chat about the event and I concluded by asking her what she meant. She answered with a chuckle, "The page, silly. You should never, ever, rip a page out of a book, Nik — especially one that I've written." June was very real!

June the Friend

A few years back, I was deliberating about asking June for advice on a professional matter. I called our mutual friend, Jim Bratton, and asked if he thought she'd mind. "Call June, Nik. She'd do anything for you." I did call her, feeling somewhat brazen to be disturbing her about something not fundraising related. She helped me see the situation in a new light. Better still, she helped me appreciate something I will never ever forget — that we were friends. She was concerned, loving, helpful, and generous with her time. June was a friend!

Perhaps that was the key to June. After all these years I've come to realize that it was never, ever, solely about her, but rather, about the collective us — all of us. She had the uncanny ability to motivate like-minded people to come together and change things for the better. Never for ourselves, but rather, for those in pain and in need.

May her work and her memory be eternal!

Nik Manojlovich is the Gemini-award winning host and co-creator of Savoir Faire, *the show that guides viewers through ways to "Make Every Day Entertaining!" He is also the past chair of Casey House Foundation. It was during his seven years as a board member of Casey House that he became friends with June Callwood.*

PATRICK CONLON

IT'S EASY TO SENTIMENTALIZE June, now that she's gone. She could be warm and generous and inclusive, behaviours her friends struggled to emulate. But she was not the cloying stuff of a Hallmark sympathy card. She could also be cranky and arch and dismissive, behaviours her friends studiously overlooked. Like the best among us, those who can stir the human heart to positive accomplishment, she evoked a quick plus/ minus calculation and won every time.

I knew June for more than thirty years, going back to when we were both CBC-TV hosts. She was already famous by then but went out of her way to welcome and support a guileless newcomer. Even then, I knew that on-camera work was a favoured career choice for barracudas and that June's effortless embrace was uncommon. We became friends.

We stayed in touch as our careers fractured and reformed, and then worked together again to help build Casey House. That's when I saw, close up, the June who could channel profound personal outrage into strategic action. All of the world's marginalized were her true children. She fought fiercely and intelligently for them, determined to level barriers with a commitment to demonstrable fairness that went far beyond glib political sloganeering.

In late 2005, I was finishing *No Need to Trouble the Heart* for Raincoast Books. It chronicles the fifteen-week hospital stay endured by Jim, my longtime partner who'd been struck suddenly with acute respiratory distress syndrome (ARDS). I was at Jim's hospital bedside for all of it, resolved from the start of the crisis to be active in his care and not just a spectator. June had taught me well.

I sent along a copy of the manuscript to June, asking if she'd consider writing a foreword but knowing her cancer was already starting to take her downhill and she had to be cautious with her time and energy. The manuscript came back in a few days with a scribbled note on the front page: "This is terrific. Yes, I'll do it but it will be short. Sorry about the stains. Orange juice. I read this in a hospital waiting room." The foreword followed within a week. It stunned me with its grace and insight. I had already pressed Raincoast to make sure June was paid for her contribution, although she and I had never discussed a fee of any kind. But I didn't want this one to be a freebie. She would honour the book with her presence in it.

Shortly before the book was published, a bunch of Casey House alumni were gathered at a party at Marg McBurney's house. June was there, elegantly dressed as always and looking frail but game. One eye on the exit, ready to bolt the moment courtesy allowed. I guess someone had made a reference to the book because I suddenly heard her hoot, loud enough to silence the room. "They paid me! I couldn't believe it! I've written lots of forewords but this is the first time I've ever been paid for one."

A little was going back to June, who never asked for it, who always gave more than she got, and I was glad.

Patrick Conlon is an award-winning journalist and broadcaster. He is the author of Sanctuary: Stories from Casey House Hospice *(Prentice-Hall, 1991), a critically acclaimed look at North America's first free-standing hospice for people with* AIDS. *He has also written* No Need to Trouble the Heart *(Raincoast Books, 2006) and* The Essential Hospital Handbook: How to Be an Effective Partner in a Loved One's Care *(Yale University Press, 2009).*

RICHARD SILVER

JUNE WAS RELENTLESS IN inspiring those around her with her many deeds, but her words held special, almost supernatural powers. We worked together during those challenging early years at Casey House.

In time, I moved away from Casey House to other community projects, but I was constantly reminded that June was keeping an eye on us and all that we were trying to accomplish.

Months, then years, would go by and from time to time I would get one of her "notes." A note from June was a huge treat — she could write an essay in a few words and you would understand, good or bad, what she was thinking and feeling. I found myself copying her on correspondence in the hope of getting a "note" back … totally selfish on my part.

I always felt that no matter what, I was and still am under June's blanket.

Richard Silver is a realtor who lives in Toronto.

JOHN LOWNSBROUGH ∽

I FIRST MET JUNE Callwood when I profiled her for a magazine called *City and Country Home*. Our first meeting took place in Casey House, though it was not yet really Casey House — the property had just recently been purchased and my subject walked me through the empty spaces talking excitedly about the AIDS hospice that was to be. Her excitement proved contagious. I ended up donating to Casey House my fee on the *City and Country Home* piece. She had that effect on people.

We stayed in touch and in the 1990s I became a member of what was then the Casey House Foundation Board. When my board term ended, she and I became lunch buddies, meeting three or four times a year, usually at Bistro 990. Fernando, Susie, and the rest of the Bistro gang plainly adored her and it was lovely being able to bask in their affection for her. Our conversations covered the waterfront, Casey House, social issues, personalities, editors we liked, and editors we didn't like. Lunch would invariably involve a couple of glasses of wine each and strong coffee. Then we would walk back up Bay Street to the parking lot at St. Basil's and she would get in her sporty black Miata convertible and drive off, the very image of indomitability.

This routine continued through the end of 2006, in other words quite a bit after her initial diagnosis with terminal cancer. She approached the matter of her own mortality with a kind of wondering bemusement and even flinty humour. If I saw weariness on those later occasions, it seemed to stem more from concern for her beloved husband — "my guy," she always called him, the delight in that exclamation palpable — and her family. I flew out to Palm Springs for a week in late February 2007 and when I arrived back in Toronto I phoned her to see about lunch. She returned my call within the week and left this message: "John Lownsbrough, I'm glad you're back and I hope you had a wonderful trip. It's June Callwood. I can't have lunch right now. I've got a leaky leg. My legs are all big, big and swollen, and one of them leaks water. A nurse comes in to change the dressings, da-dee-da-dee-dee. A week or two when this situation calms down we'll go dancing." Missing from any transcript, of course, is the warmth and cadence of that phone message, the matter-of-fact way in which, with a singsong "da-dee-da-dee-dee," she dismissed the indignities of the cancer that would claim her life in a month's time. We never spoke again, never did go dancing. I have saved and re-saved that phone message.

When I wrote that *City and Country Home* piece more

than two decades ago, I did something I hardly ever do. I broke the fourth wall, and declared my feelings for the subject. It seemed impossible not to, at least in her case. As I remember, the piece's last line went, "I suspect that to know June Callwood is to love her." Years of friendship proved those instincts correct. Intensely, irresistibly human, that's what she was. I miss her.

John Lownsbrough is an award-winning writer whose work has appeared in Toronto Life, Saturday Night, *and* Chatelaine *as well as other major magazines. His social history,* The Privileged Few: The Grange and its People in Nineteenth Century Toronto, *was shortlisted for the City of Toronto Book Award.*

DONALD MARTIN

I ADMIRED JUNE CALLWOOD. Because of her writing. Her activism. Her heart. And because she helped me understand
the importance of breathing. Yes, breathing. When I lived
in Toronto and was involved in various charities our paths
constantly crossed, and I was always taken with just how
incredibly calm she was in the spotlight, in a crowd, facing
reporters or a deadline. I noticed this about her because I was
precisely the opposite (i.e., not calm). So, one day, I asked what
her secret might be. She smiled that sunny smile of hers and
said, "I remember to breathe." It sounded so simple, almost
too simple. Like, who knew?

In 1988, when my movie *No Blame* had its world premiere
at the St. Lawrence Centre for the Arts as a gala fundraiser
for Casey House, June was there. *No Blame*, starring Helen
Shaver, was the first TV movie ever to deal with AIDS from a
woman's perspective. I was producing the evening's gala and,
thus, I was a bag of nerves. Nothing was quite going as planned.

Such events never do. June happened to walk by and said, simply, "Donald, you're not breathing." I shot her a look. With a twinkle in her eye, she took an exaggerated deep breath, like a balloon being filled with air. And, so, I did the same. We both laughed and, immediately, I felt much better. Later that evening, when I walked on stage to address the audience, I was riddled with anxiety. The first face I saw in the theatre was June's, and she silently mouthed the word *breathe*. And, so, I did. The anxiety went away. Just like that. With a single breath.

Months later, I was visiting a friend at Casey House. He died that day, in my presence. When I felt him take his last breath, it catapulted me onto an emotional roller coaster. I walked out to the porch, unsure what to do. June happened to walk by, on her way into the hospice for one reason or another, and said, simply, "Donald, you're not breathing." I shot her a look, and then I took a slow, deep breath. I didn't need to explain why I was there or what had just taken place; it's as if she knew. She wrapped her arms around me and whispered, "Breathe." And, so, I did. I breathed in her perfume. I breathed in her kindness, her strength. She matched her breaths with mine. We didn't say another word. We just breathed.

I will never forget that moment of grace. That is what it was, and that is what June Callwood was. Grace. And ever so graceful. Like a good deep breath.

Donald Martin is an award-winning screenwriter, based in Los Angeles, and the recipient of the inaugural Gemini Humanitarian Award and the Golden Jubilee Medal of Queen Elizabeth II. No Blame was his first movie. It was nominated for five Gemini Awards, won the Red Cross Award in Monte Carlo, and was screened at the Fifth International AIDS *Conference.*

PEARSE MURRAY ~

I REMEMBER THE EVENING that I first met June. It was in the early eighties, and we were at the National Ballet School on Maitland Street in Toronto. An ad hoc group of people (most of whom had never met before) had gathered to discuss the merits and countless challenges of creating a hospice for people living with AIDS.

Of course, I knew who June Callwood was — after all, I had seen that famous photograph of June being held in a police paddy wagon back in the early days of Yorkville. Here was this nice suburban lady dressed to the nines, being hauled away by Toronto's finest. I knew then that she was a woman who would fight for the underdog.

When I was finally introduced to June, the first thing I noticed about her were her fabulous legs. She had the best gams! Moreover, she radiated an aura of power and confidence. June was a born leader. Her magical charisma said, "listen to me, follow me." And we did. One of her greatest skills was the knack of finding the right people to get things done. She would look you in the eye and you were a goner — it was hard to say no to her. Despite her formidable command of the English language, she did not know the meaning of the word *impossible*.

June believed in people. She trusted me to be one of the early chairs of the Casey House Foundation and, as the years went on, we became lifelong friends. Whenever we would see each other, her first question was always, "How's your guy?" We would talk about my guy, Taras, and then we would talk about her guy, Trent. June would always have a story about Trent. Their love for each other was so apparent.

About five years ago, June brought Trent to Fort Lauderdale (prior to that she always drove down by herself — usually in her trusted Miata). I believe she had been going to Florida for over fifty years. She loved to swim in the ocean and bake in the sun. On that trip with Trent, they dropped by our home. June and I and our two guys sat by the pool feasting on shrimp and nonstop conversation. It was very special seeing their love in action. The gathering became an annual "must do" event.

Last year June was too ill to come to Florida. This did not stop our conversations. We spoke on the phone on everything from fashion to politics. And of course, Casey House was top of her agenda. One of her last marathon phone calls was to decide to whom June would gave her final interview.

When June passed, she left me a wonderful gift — the friendship of her guy Trent. He is a remarkable, witty, and generous soul. I am so pleased to have him and members of the Frayne family in my life.

Pearse Murray is a Toronto realtor. He served as chair of the Casey House Foundation board for several years.

TARAS SHIPOWICK ～

WHEN TELLING THE CASEY House story, June often referred to the "magnificent" ribbon created for the ribbon cutting ceremony during the opening of Casey House Hospice, more than twenty years ago. Why did this image continue to live on in June's memory? Like so many Casey House stories, this one is another of June's gems.

I was part of the original team of volunteers assisting to ready the house for its opening day launch. My company, Showmakers, was contributing the production resources for the week-long celebrations. At the very end of our final tie-down meeting, and just after everyone had kicked off their shoes with exhaustion, June jumped up with renewed energy and turned to me, saying, "We need a *magnificent* ribbon to mark our doorway!"

If you knew June, you knew that was a "Call to Action."

Instantly, we knew what she meant.

All agreed that the original red ribbon was simply

uninspiring, colourless, PALE. WITHOUT SIGNIFICANCE (say it) … ORDINARY! Yes, June was right again! We needed "EXTRAORDINARY." Something to ceremoniously capture the euphoric spirit that filled the room. Something that would honour the dreams and commitment shared by this unlikely group of people, brought together by a desire to make a difference.

June was right — we needed a monumental ribbon to express the enthusiasm and magnitude of this project. She suggested moving the focus of the opening ceremony to the entrance of the residence … the heart of the house. The ribbon would stay for the entire week. It would be a symbol that would inspire those who crossed the threshold — future residents, caregivers, families, supporters.

I raced back to our shop to gather whatever I had to rise to June's challenge. Bundling every colour, style, and size of ribbon, string, cord, wool I could find, I rushed back to the house for the next morning's setup.

At the archway dividing the public area from the residence, we began to construct the signature. We chose ribbons of different style and colour, to represent the diversity of each contributor and future resident: thin ribbons, fat ribbons, some shiny, some pale; rugged twill and satin silk draped next to plush velvet and sparkling glitter.

Each ribbon held its own personality but when bundled with the rest, appeared more impressive and stronger than hanging by itself.

There were short ribbons and long ones but each was able to bridge the threshold alone. Together they were abundant enough to puddle to the floor, as if trying to take root in the new carpet ... much like the old tree rooted in the front yard that became home for the resident guard dog.

In many ways it felt like we were tying an enormous bow around a gift box of dreams. Before the ceremony, the VIP's were asked to make sure all the ribbons were cut together, leaving none behind. They did so using a simple pair of scissors, which like so many things, was borrowed in haste, from a neighbour.

Although the house was now complete, the AIDS war was just beginning. We needed our ribbon to become a symbol of hope. We needed the spirit of these pioneering days to remind us that when a few dedicated dreamers come together, remarkable things can happen. This is what June taught us.

Taras Shipowick is an award-winning creative director specializing in live and mixed media productions. He is executive producer at Showmakers Inc.

MARTIN JULIEN ༶

MY FATHER, LEO JULIEN — long-time caseworker with the Children's Aid Society, former monk and forever-recovering Roman Catholic, and fan of musicals, magazines, and muscled men — was diagnosed with AIDS in 1985. I was twenty-four at the time, and my dad, at fifty-seven, was remarkably older than the scores of young men — all about my age — who were confronting this syndrome. And who were dying, at this time — without fail. Often dying in complete isolation, bereft of companionship, compassion, and humane medical care.

We, in our family, were luckier. Inspired, I believe, by the lucidity and humour of my father's fair-minded reckoning with his own mortality, we gathered around him. Slowly, at first. Respectfully, I hope. Convincingly, in the end.

He remained independent, having moved into his own bachelor apartment in the oh-so-dense-and-miraculously-diverse neighbourhood of St. Jamestown in Toronto, for the last two years of his life. We all came to visit — to cook his meals, clean his toilet, trim his beard ... and talk. Boy, did he love to talk. His observations about the human comedy in which we are all characters were penetrating, sensitive, wicked, and merciful. And ... okay, it's true: merciless. He could be relentless in his insight; unforgiving in his careful and loving dissection of human folly and hubris. In himself, of course, as well as others. Hmm. So. That reminds me of June Callwood.

For the first three of his last five weeks of life, he lived at Mt. Sinai Hospital, where we all did the best we could. Including the nurses. We started keeping a journal by Leo's bedside about our visits. So many visitors he had! Many patients on the isolated "AIDS ward" — those young men beset by lesions and shame — had no visitors at all. This was 1988.

And we waited, and hoped, and negotiated, and ... waited ... and waited ... for the new hospice, Casey House, to open. And my father knew ... and waited. And hung on. And became sicker. And less lucid. And much, much thinner. And he had good days. And bad days.

He had known June for years. A bit peripherally — but closely, too. He had been a founding member of PWA (People with AIDS) Toronto. June mentions him in *Jim: A Memoir*, her book about the early HIV/AIDS activist Jim St. James. Leo comes off as a bit provocative: intelligent, curious, compassionate — yet slyly disruptive. Hmm. So. That reminds me of June, too.

My dad got into Casey House that spring. He was the second resident. And the second person to die there, two weeks after his arrival, just shy of his sixtieth birthday. He was surrounded by his ex-wife (and my mother) Marion, her partner Sylvia, Marion's mother (my grandmama!), also named Marion, my partner Shery, his great friends John and Clark — and many others. And the staff of Casey House, still so new and trembling and marvelous. And June, of course; the spirit of June Callwood, so palpable in every breath we took. In every breath that sometimes ceased.

I see my father in his palliative bed at Casey House. Serene, smiling, his withered and translucent hands clasped on his tiny blanketed lap, looking out the window of his splendid room. "Oh, this is where I belong. This really is my home and ... oh! I'm so happy here! Thank you all for having me!"

And that reminds me of June, too.

Martin Julien is an actor and playwright who lives in Toronto. Perhaps his deepest sadness is that his sons, Lucas and Truman, never got to know their amazing grandfather, Leo Julien.

JANE DARVILLE ～

I WAS FORTUNATE TO know June from the mid eighties when I attended one of the first meetings to discuss a free-standing hospice for people living with AIDS. From then until her death I learned a lot from observing June as she conducted her life. These "learnings" are too many to write about in this remembrance but here are the ones that immediately come to mind.

I was asked to attend an early meeting of the aforementioned hospice committee to review the Home Care Program (HCP) and determine if there was an option for HCP involvement in the provision of care. I never left this committee. This was the thing about June: if you had something worthwhile to offer the process you were in the game for the long term. You never said no to her and your life was enhanced for this.

One of my strongest memories of June was at a meeting once we knew the location of the hospice. We thought there might be some community resistance and had a planning session to determine what we would say to the neighbours as we individually went door to door to introduce ourselves and the hospice. It was a long and late meeting. As always, June was right in there working through the issues with the full knowledge that she would join us that evening. June never acted as the honorary member of the committee. She was always there in the middle of the work, doing the work.

The last time I saw June was at a lunch at the home of Margaret McBurney about a month or so before she died. It was in March and she was off to the last appointment with her oncologist. As she said at the time, "This is my last appointment with the oncologist; I have graduated to palliative care." It was also just a day or so before her last interview, which was at her home, with George Stroumboulopoulos. She liked his youth and energy and was looking forward to meeting him. In that interview she spoke passionately of how kindness would save the world — little kindnesses like opening the door for someone, smiling as you walked past people on the street. At the end of the televised interview she smiled at George and said something to the effect that he was good at his job. June never let an opportunity go by to compliment someone or be kind. In remembrance of June I now take a breath when I feel myself becoming impatient as I go about my day so I don't get snappy with salespeople and waiters who are just doing their job and trying to be helpful. I remember that these small kindnesses will save the world.

I also learned from observing June that if you have good legs that are slightly tanned you can wear skirts and dresses and "go with naked legs" well into the autumn.

Thanks June.

Jane Darville is a senior healthcare administrator and consultant. She was on the Steering Committee and Founding Board of Casey House and was its executive director from 1990 to 1994. She has lived and worked in Ontario and British Columbia. She currently lives in Toronto with her partner, Dr. Skip Bassford, whom she met when they were both on the Board of Casey House Hospice.

CAMPAIGN AGAINST CHILD POVERTY

*Over one million children in this country wake up
every day in poverty. They have to count on us to make
decisions in this election that will improve their futures.*

— JUNE CALLWOOD

PEDRO BARATA ~

IN THE EARLY 2000S, I worked at Campaign 2000 — the firebrand coalition that refuses to let governments off the hook for child poverty. June Callwood was a regular, driving fixture there. She used to co-chair our sister organization, the Campaign Against Child Poverty.

June's unflinching commitment to social justice is legendary, and we in the child poverty movement all learned much from her — lessons that continue to apply today:

- The invaluable quality of dogged determination and of telling yourself and others that, no matter what the circumstances, you're not quitting and you will persevere.
- The importance of humanity, of understanding social ills by establishing meaningful connections with those who go through rough times.
- The balance between passion and evidence in how you tell your story.

And of course, she taught us the secret weapon of knowing how to mingle. June knew better than anybody how to manoeuvre a social event. In the midst of the Harris years in the nineties, June would often come back from a social event, ready to unlock doors that seemed to have been previously nailed shut for us social advocates. "I was chatting with Janet Ecker the other night," she would say nonchalantly about her run-in with the minister of education. "I told her we were coming to talk to her about the link between a good education and the scourge of child poverty."

Another day it might be Jim Flaherty, minister of finance, or some other senior official who look on in puzzlement as those people from the bad press clippings came waltzing through the doors of power on the coattails of Saint June.

Sometimes it actually paid off.

Paul Martin, former prime minister and minister of finance, was a huge June Callwood fan and laid out the welcome mat to June and company on many occasions. I'd like to think those conversations had something to do with the major investments made in one of Canada's most successful antipoverty programs — the Canada Child Tax Benefit — and even that briefly lived national childcare program that died shortly after Martin's Liberals were unseated in 2006.

Ontario Premier Dalton McGuinty was a fan too. A few months prior to the 2007 provincial budget, social justice activists and community groups learned that the province was considering the introduction of a new Ontario Child Benefit as one of many possible cornerstones for the budget. We all took a deep breath and decided this was an opportunity that could not be missed. Yes, the campaigns already on the ground were still important; yes, our principled multifaceted agendas and demands would continue to be pushed; and yes, there was plenty of skepticism. But we also knew that child benefits are among the most critical tools in the fight against child poverty. In jurisdictions where child poverty is lowest, a generous child benefit program is invariably present families supplement their paycheques. So a variety of groups — such as the Daily Bread Food Bank, Campaign 2000 and the Campaign Against Child Poverty, the Atkinson Foundation, the Caledon Institute, the Income Security Advocacy Centre, the Toronto City Summit Alliance, the Interfaith Social Assistance Reform Coalition, and the Ontario Registered Nurses — signed on to an endorsement of the Ontario Child Benefit approach that provided the government with the support it would need to initiate a major, and very expensive, antipoverty program.

Like all things of this nature, there were a few bumps along the way.

There was a lot of hard work, much to-and-fro-ing, negotiating and finding middle ground. At one point, our fledgling coalition of coalitions seemed to have hit a roadblock in our discussions with government. It jeopardized all we had worked for. So, there was only one thing to do. We called June. Would she meet with the premier?

At the other end of the phone line, that woman who had

already accomplished and given so much, and who now found herself slowed down by a tough battle with terminal cancer, did not hesitate. "Let's do it," she said. "Bill will drive me."

June and the premier had a long chat. They talked about life, death, growing up, struggling in a big family, and standing up for the right thing. By the end of the meeting, our work was back on track and the Ontario Child Benefit eventually found its way into the budget — with more of a kick than what may have first been expected. Some of the language in the eventual budget, especially the part about how all children will benefit — whether their parents are working or on social assistance — was there in no small part thanks to June (and of course, definitely the premier).

She was amazing. A pragmatic idealist, an incredibly resourceful human being, incessantly determined and optimistic almost to a fault. And she got things done in the process.

June's not here anymore to kick those doors down. It's up to us to carry that legacy. And I don't have to tell you there's plenty of work to do.

Pedro Barata is Director of Public Affairs at United Way Toronto, and has also worked with Family Service Toronto, Campaign 2000, and the Atkinson Foundation.

ARLENE PERLY RAE

ALTHOUGH I KNEW HER for a long time — in several ways and different contexts — my best memories of June come from many years of collaboration on the Campaign Against Child Poverty (CACP).

She was a stalwart, our best worker, and our muse. She worked long and hard for the cause, spoke about it often in speeches and interviews, and pressured political leaders at every level and at every opportunity to make a difference.

She would zoom up to the (often early morning) meetings of the core group of CACP activists in her little convertible, dressed perfectly, and perfectly coiffed. But make no mistake, she was there on business. June was sunny, but tough. She had gentle but persuasive ways to prod and pressure, to push and embarrass our business leaders and governments to act, to give, to do something, whatever was in their hearts and in their power, to help alleviate the problem, and to keep doing so. She was able to exercise the magic of those calls and visits — from her formidable Rolodex database — over and over. Somehow, through her charm, winning personality, and charisma, she managed never to wear out her welcome. They took her calls again and again, and as often as not, responded to her pleas for help.

There are many who believe June took their cause more seriously than any of her others. They all mattered to her too, and she, with tireless energy, worked for many good things. But I am convinced that she cared about young mothers and babies, people with HIV/AIDS, and poor children and families, more than anything else and more than anyone else I have ever known.

She was a wonderful writer, an amazing advocate, and besottedly and forever in love with her "Bill," Trent Frayne, all their many years together. She was funny, irreverent, gutsy, and indefatigable.

She never got over losing their son, Casey. She took the news of her cancer stoically and with a serenity most of us cannot imagine. She was a unique mentor and a hero — to me and to many others.

I miss her every day.

Arlene Perly Rae is a writer and speaker. Her particular interest is advocacy on behalf of young people, including literacy, mental health, child poverty, and the arts.

CAROLINE MORGAN DI GIOVANNI ⟋

OF ALL THE MANY, many people she knew and worked with, I was probably one of the latecomers. June and I were together on the steering committee of the Campaign Against Child Poverty, starting in 1998. That is when I first sat with her on a working group, and saw her in action at meetings and as a speaker on behalf of children and families living below the poverty line. June was our champion. She showed no fear at speaking truth to power, to the point where power sometimes showed fear when they saw her approaching. For the rest of us on the committee, her tireless commitment was the prod that kept us going. If she could be up and perfectly dressed, cheerful and dynamic at a breakfast meeting with the Rotary Club, then we could be too, by golly; no excuses allowed. She lived that way, and motivated others that way.

When she informed the committee, at one of our eight a.m. meetings, that she "had cancer, and so could we please change the next meeting from Wednesday to Thursday because she had a doctor's appointment," we were astonished by the news, but not surprised at her attitude. Her cancer would be regarded as an inconvenience. We were all to carry on, stronger than ever. The thought of children going to bed hungry and homeless in our rich country drove her to action. She never backed down, not even in her last weeks, in hospital. She accepted a visit from Premier Dalton McGuinty the day the Ontario Child Benefit was announced in the budget speech. From her bedside she challenged him to continue to make improvements in the lives of children.

In my own way, I got to know and admire June as a role model. I went home from the meeting when she told us of her illness, and sent her this poem by email. Of course, she responded graciously, as she did to so many others. Best of all she zeroed in on the very lines in the poem that were inspired by her:

"Somersaulting Man: As I Think of Myself"
Stone carving by John Kavik, 1964. AGO

Tumbling backwards
face
full of joy

free to fly
nearly
earthbound, but

free

> *spirit free*

> > *free to tumble over*

flexible, but

> *balanced*

> > *on only*

> > > *two hands*

The centre holds

> *eyes open*

> > *energetic*

suddenly

> *arrested*

As others think of you
"As I think of

> *my*

> > *self."[1]*

Caroline Morgan Di Giovanni is a writer and editor who grew up in Philadelphia and came to Toronto in 1966 to attend

---

1   Based on a stone carving by John Kavik, 1964. Art Gallery of Ontario. From Caroline Morgan Di Giovanni's book *Looking at Renaissance Paintings and Other Poems* (Quattro Books, 2008). Used by permission of the author.

St. Michael's College at the University of Toronto. She married Alberto Di Giovanni in 1972 and has lived in Toronto ever since, serving as a school board trustee, then a municipal councillor, and a community volunteer. She fell in love with poetry as a young child and in adolescence discovered theatre. These two literary forms provide the channel for all her creative energy. Fortunately, she chose to live in Canada and contribute whole-heartedly to the cultural life of this country. Website: www. quattrobooks.ca

JUNE'S FRIENDS

If people were kinder, they would be happier.
If they were happier, more people would be kindly.
If more people were happy, the world would be kinder.
If the world were kinder, it might survive.

— JUNE CALLWOOD

VALERIE PRINGLE ❦

LIKE SO MANY PEOPLE, I worshipped June. She was one of my heroes and role models. I interviewed her many times and had a few great lunches with her in the last two years of her life. I remember her telling me at the Casey House party in honour of her eightieth that she was having hot flashes because she had to go off her hormones due to cancer treatments. After my mother died, I told June I wanted her to be my mother. I have a speech I give about the five people I interviewed who most impressed and influenced me. June is one of them.

June Callwood was very different. She's was not so cocksure. I admired her and her lifelong activism and passion and compassion. I was impressed by how she handled her cancer and what seemed like impending death, although she looked terrific. At eighty-two she said "all of us are groping all the time to figure out what kind of person we're going to be," and "I've always thought that next year I'll be wise. I've never minded growing old because next year is the year…. I'm still waiting for homeostasis, when everything is in sync. It hasn't happened." Like Leonard Cohen's line about enlightenment and lightening up, June said to have grace you have to have gratitude. She believed that everyone has a huge load of sadness and that no one gets through this veil of tears without losses that are unbearable and she has certainly had those. She went on: "you have to figure out what it is you will not tolerate — and I will not tolerate indifference to something I think is unjust. You must interfere and it's the interfering that keeps us together as a society. We must look after one another. And not just family and friends but strangers as well. I believe passionately in that." She quoted Santayana that "life is not a spectacle or a feast … it's a predicament." And T.S. Eliot, "For us there is only the trying, the rest is not our business." She was proud that she didn't quit, that she kept trying. She said "You set yourself not on a goal but on a journey. You give it your best shot. I'm lucky that I have that philosophy, but a lot of goals elude me."

I loved the way she ended her essay on old age in the anthology *Dropped Threads*: "I'm a work in progress. I always thought that when I got old I would have the answers to the imponderable questions surrounding human existence. So far, that's not how it's turning out. Oh well." I love that *Oh well*. What can you do? That's the balance. The profound and the realistic.

The other thing I always remembered her saying — ad libbed — was at a fundraiser for Flora MacDonald when she ran for the leadership of the federal PCs. You don't think of June as a Tory, but she explained that it was important for her to be there to support women in leadership roles, because, she went on, "last night my daughter was staying at my house with her baby and I woke to sounds of crying and stumbled in my nightgown, past all the sleeping men, to pick up the child. Women are the ones who hear the sounds of crying in the night. That's why we need one to be prime minister." It was brilliant.

Valerie Pringle is a broadcaster and volunteer. She is a Member of the Order of Canada.

ELIZABETH GRAY

IN THE CLOSING MONTHS of 1996, some public-spirited Torontonians launched a campaign to save the CBC. They included such luminaries as philanthropist Jack Rabinovitch, broadcaster Andy Barrie, activist Arlene Perly Rae, and, of course, June Callwood, this country's acknowledged champion of worthy causes, hopeless or otherwise.

Convinced that budget cuts planned by the Chretien government would destroy the public broadcaster, they believed the only hope lay in mobilizing public opinion. Nothing less than a national campaign would do, and so they devised one and they called it "CBC ... Ours to Keep!"

The goal of "Ours to Keep!", they decided, would be a petition of one million signatures gathered from across the country and borne triumphantly to Ottawa by April of the following year.

Committees were duly struck from coast to coast, each with a provincial or territorial captain charged with organizing grassroots volunteers. The *Toronto Star* publisher of the day, John Honderich, donated an office in the newspaper's downtown building ... and "Ours to Keep!" had a national headquarters.

Volunteers quickly filled desks, banging on typewriters and burning up phone lines. This was before email; the phone bill was staggering. From Gibsons Landing to Whitehorse to Yellowknife to St. John's, signatures were gathered and counted ... and gathered and counted.

In Toronto, as the campaign began to take on a life of its own, most of the original founders quietly withdrew, limiting their support to occasional meetings, leaving the daily rough and tumble to the volunteers. Not June. This was where she shone. Canada's most seasoned campaigner was in her element.

She was always dropping in, offering invaluable advice, calling influential people — the ones who normally never return phone calls but who were flattered to talk to Callwood. She doled out encouragement like popcorn. She never forgot to give people credit.

And then there was the day she burst into the office, exploding radiance. "I have had the most wonderful day! Let me tell you about my perfect day," she beamed, flinging herself into a straight-backed chair and commanding the whole room. "I sold the screen rights to my last book a while ago and the cheque arrived today. And it's a good cheque! And I went to see Margaret Gibson and there they were, she and her partner, in despair. She's trying to write and they've spent her last advance and they can't pay the rent. And they're about to be evicted. And I was able to give them two months' rent because I had that cheque. Just like that! And after that, I still had lots left over so I went and put a down-payment on a house for Barney. It's specially designed for people with disabilities. He can manage by himself in his wheelchair ...

"Now, how are things going here? What can I do? I can type quite well, you know ... and I'm pretty good on the phone ... I don't mind stuffing envelopes ... how about some muffins from the *Star* cafeteria?"

It was a bitterly cold day and as she sat there, her long, gorgeous legs elegantly crossed, I remember noticing that that they were bare and very tanned and that all she had on her feet was a pair of cheeky black pumps.

Elizabeth Gray is a journalist/broadcaster who considers it a piece of extraordinary good fortune that she got to know June Callwood during the "Ours to Keep!" campaign. And that they remained friends for the rest of June's life.

SALLY ARMSTRONG ✑

LIKE LEGIONS OF HER other close friends, I used to treasure the lunches June and I had at a little bistro near her home. They'd started as assignment meetings while I was editor-in-chief at *Homemaker's Magazine* and soon became repasts of activism, delicious gossip, and profound trusting friendship. My treasured memories of this remarkable woman are mostly centred in her fearlessness when it came to tackling the nasty realities society preferred to ignore. For example, in 1996, June and seven other women met at a breakfast meeting at *Homemaker's* to discuss the silo system around breast cancer and the need to open a resource centre that would bring all the players together — the surgeons and oncologists, the survivors and researchers. When one woman asked where the centre could be housed, June spoke up: "We'll buy a house." The astonished breakfast group gasped and said, "But that would cost a million dollars here in downtown Toronto." June didn't blink. "Exactly — then they'll know we're serious," she said. Willow: The Breast

Cancer Resource and Support Centre opened its doors six months later, albeit in a rental facility.

One day while driving along the Gardiner Expressway in Toronto, I spotted her little Mazda Miata, top down, zipping along in the outside lane, her hair blowing in the wind, her dazzling smile telling me she was in the midst of an animated conversation with an old friend. It was an enviable scene — two women chatting under the sun, sharing their stories. Or so it seemed. When I saw her later and remarked on the serene sight, she replied, "Oh, that's a friend of mine. She's mentally deranged and tried to kill her landlord. I was driving her to the hospital for treatment."

The irrepressible June (or Joon as she sometimes signed her emails) is perhaps best remembered as a friend to almost everyone she ever met — even those who met her remotely through a magazine article or a television show. She was there for you when you were in trouble, when there was something to celebrate; she never forgot an anniversary. Her honesty, her empathy, her devastating wit were the tools she used for a lifetime of writing, broadcasting, caregiving, advocating.

That's why sitting down to lunch with June Callwood was never about being part of a twosome. Oh, she'd hear you out if you were there with a gripe, or suss you out if whatever happened to be eating you didn't spill onto the table. And she'd share the bones she'd been picking over in her own life, as friends do. But the thing about June was she didn't come to lunch alone. Her constant companions were ever-present.

Before the menu had even arrived, she'd be hunched over the table talking about a person who was sick or sad, or a community disgrace like child poverty or homelessness, or a health catastrophe like AIDS or breast cancer; and she'd be asking, "What are we going to do about it?" And her family, her daughters and son, her lifelong partner, her "sparkling grandchildren," and her beloved Casey were sprinkled throughout the meal as well. She wore her causes and her clan like a second skin. It's who she was. Put her in a room full of people with energy for action and compassion for humankind and her twinkling eyes and hearty laughter would let you know she was in her element. Her infectious can-do attitude and her crusty who-says-so denial of naysayers were part of the Callwood package. That's why she received the love of a nation and more awards and citations than anyone could keep track of. That's why people in trouble wanted her at the table. But that's not all you got at lunch. The salad of June Callwood's life came with sugar and spice all right. But it also came with the treasured gift she had of making everyone at the table feel they'd been well fed.

When she received the Lifetime Achievement Award from the Canadian Journalism Foundation in 2004, chair John Fraser said, "June Callwood has often been called the conscience of Canada. She's much more than that. She is also emblematic of its heart and soul. Her causes, her integrity, her anger, her aspirations have all become part of the definition of what it is to be a responsible, caring Canadian."

Pragmatic to the core, gentle to a fault, outspoken to the max, this country Canada has been well served by citizen June.

Sally Armstrong is an Amnesty International award winner, a Member of the Order of Canada, a documentary filmmaker, a teacher, a human rights activist, and a contributing editor at Maclean's *magazine.*

PLUM JOHNSON ⁓

JUNE CALLWOOD HAD A knack for inspiring people to "do better." But June's "doing better" didn't mean "getting more," it meant "giving more" — by thinking bigger and figuring out how to contribute effectively. Organizing and amassing the troops and then inspiring them to a common purpose — that's how I think of June.

I remember the first time I met her. I had recently started the parenting newspaper, KidsToronto, and we were seated together at a fundraiser down at Harbourfront. I marvelled at her ability to be everywhere at once, involved in so many community and charitable events. I was able to tell June how much I admired her. She brushed it off, in her characteristic style. "Anybody can do it," she said.

In 1986, June wrote a book called *Twelve Weeks in Spring* — an account of how she and a team of friends cared for Margaret Fraser at home, in her final days.

Five years later, my forty-two-year-old brother, Sandy, was

hospitalized and diagnosed with cancer. One day we were told that he had been taken to the "palliative care" ward. I was in shock, and asked the nurse what she meant. She took me to her office, handed me a box of Kleenex, and proceeded to explain. What happened next was because we had read June's book.

We borrowed a wheelchair from the nurses' station, went into the ward, surreptitiously packed Sandy's things, told the nurses we were "going for a walk," wheeled him out to the parking lot, put him in the car, and drove him home.

We found a doctor willing to make house calls, we set up a twenty-four-hour shift schedule for family members, plugged into the VON, got a home morphine pump, organized a log-in book beside his bed — in short, we followed June's recipe for a loving care-in. We didn't know how long we had (it turned out we had a little longer than sixteen weeks), but Sandy's final days included sunshine on the veranda overlooking the lake, familiar sights, sounds, and smells of his own home, daily massages by familiar hands, and a coming together of family in the most profound of experiences.

Because of *Twelve Weeks in Spring*, my brother died at home, surrounded by family and cared for by all of us. June blazed the trail — even in this — and what a gift she gave us! Her book gave us the first idea, then the knowledge and, finally, the confidence to follow her example. June's words gave us courage. "Anybody can do it," she said — and so we did. Thank you, June.

Plum Johnson is an author and a professional portrait painter. Her works are in private collections in Canada, the U.S., and Europe. She lives in Toronto.

MARGARET LYONS

IN THE SUMMER OF Love, Yorkville was the magnet for young people running from authority, from oppressive parents, and from school to celebrate freedom and look for music and poetry.

Fearful parents looked at the unkempt mob of young people on television and silently cheered the police who were dragging off the ringleaders.

June Callwood is remembered for trying to bring some sense into the scene by siding with the young victims who were only enjoying the crowd into the late night in a middle-class neighbourhood not yet used to coffee houses and clubs.

A few blocks away in a rundown late-Victorian house, she was also operating Digger House, one of her earliest shelters for the waifs and strays of a society that did not know how to cope with its rebels. It was here that some of the youngsters from the Yorkville scene looked for shelter.

My daughter Ruth was one of those runaways. That spring she was expelled from Forest Hill Collegiate for skipping class to attend a Raymond Souster poetry reading downtown with some classmates. It did not help that she had earlier tried to bring up the works of Leonard Cohen in her English class, where contemporary CanLit was unheard of. For her, this was the last straw. She wanted no more of high school, and no more of the parents who tried to persuade her to stay in school or thought a tidy room was more important than self-expression. And she disappeared.

Fortunately for her and for us, she landed in Digger House. There, under June Callwood's influence, or her buried middle-class preference for some order, she became a volunteer, some sort of house monitor. To our great relief, she turned up one day to let us know she was well and to vent her disgust at some of the habits of her peers at Digger House. "They turned the place into a pigsty," she claimed — quite innocent of the echoes of the same words that had goaded her into rebellion only a few months earlier.

June had helped a bruised young person land on her feet by quiet example, as she went on to do for so many others.

Margaret Lyons is a retired broadcasting executive, who served as Vice-President of the English Radio Networks for the CBC. *She introduced* This Country in the Morning; As It Happens; *and* Quirks and Quarks *to radio listeners in Canada. As a lifelong admirer of June Callwood, Margaret has served tirelessly in many volunteer positions. She holds an Hon. D. Litt. from McMaster University and has been named to the Order of Canada*

JOHN SEWELL

I'VE KNOWN JUNE SINCE the late 1960s. I remember the famous evening when the kids sat down on Yorkville Avenue to protest city council turning it into a one-way street. This was a few years before I became an alderman on Toronto City Council, but as a young lawyer with a progressive political outlook, it was obvious I'd be involved. June was there because of her interest in the kids: from the time of the arrests in the early evening until the sun came up next morning, she and I drove around to all the police stations in the central city to document the names of the dozens of kids the police had arrested that night, and the charges they faced.

Of course, we kept running into each other over the next forty years. I continually marvelled at her inventiveness. She was the original social entrepreneur. When, in early January 2007, I learned she was very ill, I decided to write her a note. I recounted how I was riding my bicycle down Parliament Street and passed Jessie's, the home she established for teenage mothers, and how it made me think of her and the amazingly positive influence she has had on city life. I thanked her for the profound changes she had made and wished her well.

June would have none of it. She wanted to turn the tables with a Dear John letter, on her simple letterhead — a plain "June Callwood" on an ivory-coloured page with a ragged bottom — dated January 31, 2007.

Dear John:

I picture you these bitter cold days, riding your bicycle with your principles as firmly wrapped about you as a scarf.

Whatever motivated you to write, your warm and eloquent letter could not have come at a better time. It is bad enough to be working my way through terminal cancer, without having to face February as well.

I appreciate your note beyond measure. One of the memories I have of you was during the fight for South of St. James[town], and thank God you won that one. A group of us had gathered somewhere, all of us standing while we worked through some snag, and your mother was there. You were doing the talking, passionate and convincing as always, and she had such a look of pride on her face. I thought, "Lucky John. Lucky her too."

You never give up. You should get standing ovations wherever you go. I'm giving you one right now.

> With affection and gratitude.
> June

Such a powerful and infectious spirit. She's not a woman you can say goodbye to.

John Sewell is a former mayor of Toronto.

GALE ZOË GARNETT

I FIRST MET THE extraordinary combination of determination and grace that was June Callwood when I was twenty-two and dating a *Toronto Star* journalist, the late Alexander Ross. Sandy had a nine-year-old son, Darby, who looked like the Little Prince and had the same "visitor from another planet" otherness and intelligence. He also had bone cancer.

June, who thought many adults were good, but that children and babies were best, would frequently visit Darby at Sandy's. I was usually there.

It was 1972. I'd been out of the country during June's famous 1968 Yorkvillian journey to jail, but, like most young women in Toronto, knew her justice-seeking writing and public activities. Getting to know June while Darby Ross fought his good fight, and having no family of my own, she became the woman I wanted to be when I grew up.

Not my mother. That position was fully booked. June had a family she loved, and while she was reflexively maternal with all young people, family was family. Friends, even very dear friends were extra-familial.

My favourite example of June's ad hoc mothering happened at The Half-and-Half Show, a performance fundraiser for Maggie's, a drop-in centre and peer support group for Toronto's sex-trade workers. June co-founded Maggie's. A full-bodied young woman was on the stage of the Bathurst Theatre doing her act; a musically accompanied strip-down to a turquoise satin G-string, while reading her doctoral thesis on Herbert Marcuse.

Dance and dialectic concluded, the woman left the stage. June Callwood came up from the audience, thanked us all for being there, and announced that there would be a fifteen-minute interval before act two. She encouraged our using this period to buy buttons and copies of *The Bad Trick Sheet* (a safety publication that Maggie's produced). Then, when most of the audience had headed out, June picked up the discarded clothes of about five strippers and headed up to the dressing room, folding garments as she went.

June Callwood founded or co-founded over fifty organizations. The ones in which or for which we worked together included Maggie's, Jessie's, Nellie's, PEN Canada, the Writers' Union of Canada, and Casey House. Until the last weeks of her life, June was defending the rights of others. PEN Canada called a conference to protest the banning of *My Three Wishes* (by award-winning children's book author Deborah Ellis) from some schools. June was, at least medically, quite ill, but there she was on the dais, speaking out alongside librarians, writers Edeet Ravel and Lawrence Hill, and publisher Patsy Aldana. "Book banning in the twenty-first century?!" June said incredulously, shaking her head. "I thought we stopped doing that in the 1950s!" In March, she accepted the Distinguished Contribution award from the Writers' Trust of Canada, telling all of us "when you see something that needs doing, do it."

June was married to and profoundly in love with the same man, sportswriter Trent Frayne, for over sixty years. Some called him "Trent," others called him "Bill." I once asked June what she called him. Without hesitating, she replied, "Dreamy. I call him Dreamy." She did. I heard her do it. Only when directly addressing him. Ever the professional journalist, she called him "my husband, Trent Frayne" or simply Trent Frayne when speaking of him on the record. June Callwood and Trent Frayne were one of the few married couples that made sense to me. Without making any sort of fuss or display, they simply and deeply loved each other. Over the years, when people (including June) would ask why I didn't marry, my reply was always "because I've not met my Trent Frayne or my Bill Whitehead (life-partner of the late Timothy Findley)."

We lunched together regularly for years, catching up on events, both personal and sociopolitical. June always said it was her turn to pay the bill. I finally started keeping a written record so that I could buy lunch. When she saw the little notebook, she got that I had to pay my share. After that, we properly took turns. In 1999, when I received a huge advance for my first novel, she rang, offered congratulations, and said, "You wanna buy the next lunch?" "No," I replied, "it's your turn." We both laughed. And bought lunches in the proper order. From 1982 on, these lunches always ended with me transferring books and clothing from my car to hers for the young single mums at Jessie's.

I've never met June and Trent's eldest son, Brant. I did not know Casey, whose motorcycle accident-death June mourned every day (and for whom she named Casey House, the AIDS hospice that has meant so much to so many. Invited to Christmas dinner at the Callwood-Frayne house in Islington, I met Jill Frayne and Jesse Manchester, June's two daughters. Jesse is married to Mark Manchester, with whom I've worked in films. Mark is a grip — and one of the best-looking guys on any set. At Christmas dinner, we gently teased Mark about how most of the women and some of the men with whom he worked had silent, discreet crushes on him. As with June, who was a great beauty at all ages, Mark just "had that thing" and, like June, didn't seem to think about it or fuss with it.

He also partnered with Jesse in giving June her dearly beloved grandchildren. As noted, the biggest room in June Callwood's heart full of big rooms was the one for children and babies. Along with a commitment to active advocacy, it is June's commitment to children that has taken most deeply in me.

Literature for Life, a group that works for and with single mums and their children, and is centred on writing and reading to your kids, grew out of Jessie's. Jo Altilia runs for Lit4Life.

I am its ad hoc Writer in Residence. I've also initiated, with support and aid from both the Writers' Union of Canada and the Stephen Lewis Foundation, the CanadAfricaKidLit BookLift (Canadian Children's Books for the students at the Nyaka AIDS Orphans' School in Uganda). When June heard about this, she said "Damn! I wish I'd written a children's book to give you." I remember being described once, in a newspaper caption from a rally, as "actor, writer, and activist." Seeing the word "activist" next to my name, I called it my June Award. Just a word. A small accomplishment but a great honour.

There's been, since her passing, a lot of "Saint June" talk. June Callwood was not a saint. She was a worker. If you disagreed, she expected you, without shouting or name-calling, to fight in your corner. She genuinely listened. Sometimes compromise could be found. When it couldn't, there would always, at the least, be clarity. June was a first-rate journalist and clarity went with the job description.

June Callwood gave more, to more, more steadily than anyone I've ever known (and I know a number of people with the action gene). Alongside with the ocean of giving that was June Callwood, we each periodically hold aloft our thimbleful of water. I heard the news on Saturday morning and went to Casey House. There were many people there. Some of us wrote in the June Book. Some spoke with others. Leaving, I saw that the lawn had filled with flowers and notes.

We were enriched because June was here. We are lessened because she is gone. She did leave a map. We can use her map.

We can build her map. It is a huge map — lots of room for building. So, when you see something that needs doing, do it. June Callwood and the many for whom she worked deserve nothing less.

Gale Zoe Garnett is a writer, a member of the Writers' Union of Canada, an actor, and an activist.

ALISON GORDON ✍

JUNE CALLWOOD WAS NOT a potty mouth. Elegantly articulate, she had no need to resort to profanity most of the time. But under duress, she wasn't afraid to reach into the most forceful part of her vocabulary.

And she was most definitely under duress on that evening in September 1989 when she uttered the "fuck off" heard around the world — or at least around Greater Metropolitan Toronto — to the handful of misguided and self-righteous protesters who accosted her outside Roy Thomson Hall.

Some amount of background information might be in order here. June was, at that point, the incoming president of PEN Canada, a branch of the international organization that works on behalf of imprisoned writers and freedom of expression worldwide. Though still a relatively small organization they had just pulled off a tremendous feat. In partnership with PEN Quebec, with the assistance of a handful of overworked staff and volunteers, PEN Canada had just organized the single most accessible and diverse International PEN Congress in the organization's history. They had gone hat in hand to corporate sponsors, bullied their publishers, twisted arms in government bureaucracies, and generally busted their collective asses to ensure that, for the first time since the organization was founded in 1926, it was a truly representative gathering.

There were as many female as male delegates, there was representation from every continent, every race. There was representation of aboriginal peoples. The PEN group had even arranged for some of the visiting writers to visit the far north. And, finally, the congress, the first ever to be conducted trilingually in English, French, and Spanish, was going to be packed up — lock, stock, and delegates — and put on a train to Montreal for the second half.

It was, in short, a triumph for PEN Canada. They had given a good hard democratizing shake to a group that had for too long been dominated by European males. They were, justifiably, pretty proud of themselves.

And then, virtually on the eve of the Congress, an ad hoc group called Vision 21 showed up out of nowhere with an astonishing accusation: PEN Canada is a racist organization.

The group was media savvy and their press release received considerable coverage. More importantly, in those early days of political correctness, it was virtually unquestioned. It wasn't up to Vision 21 to prove that PEN Canada was racist; it was up to PEN Canada to prove it was not.

So this was the "when-did-you-stop-beating-your-wife"

scenario that June found herself in when she left the gala opening concert for congress delegates and PEN supporters on that September evening. From what I understand from people closer to the centre of things, the protesters had been repeatedly invited to come inside and meet the multiracial gathering of delegates, but had refused — disinclined, one must surmise, to be "co-opted by the enemy."

They had handed leaflets to guests arriving and were standing by to do the same at the end of the evening. June was among the early departures, with her husband, Trent Frayne. As it happened, I left at about the same time, with a group, and was close enough to hear her brush the protesters off as they offered her the leaflets.

"Fuck off," she said.

And, under the circumstances, who could blame her?

And that was that. Or should have been.

Have I already mentioned that the group was media-savvy? They certainly were savvy enough to make an immediate phone call to *The Globe and Mail* to report that *Saint June Callwood* had told them to fuck off.

And the person on the desk at the *Globe*, or the person who that person called to consult, however high up the line that went, decided that this was front-page news.

June, mind you, was one of their own. She had worked for the paper for years, and was still, I believe, a contributor at the time. Frayne's column still ran in the sports section, if memory serves. Did that give them no pause? Or, more ominously, was that why the decision was made — to get rid of a troublesome colleague, a woman whose politics were pinker than theirs? Or were they simply worried that if they didn't print it, they'd be tarred with the same racist brush? Whatever the motivation, the decision was made.

And, according to June, they never even called to check the story's accuracy with her. Not that she would have denied it. But it would have been nice, not to mention journalistically ethical, to have her provide a bit of context as she saw it. And it would have been only civilized to have provided her a bit of warning about the shit flying towards the fan.

The incident was upsetting enough on its own. June felt very badly about the negative publicity she had inadvertently brought down around PEN's ears. But the cruelest aspect of the whole stupid controversy was that somehow June's very name became bracketed, in the minds of some, with the original unfounded accusation: June Callwood, Racism. Anyone who knew her understood that June was as close to colour-blind as is humanly possible. But reality didn't enter into it.

So when June later resigned from the board of Nellie's — a home for abused women that she had founded, for heaven's sake — there was talk. Because the resignation had come after disagreements with some staff and board members who were women of colour, there was inevitably muttering about "well, you know, that PEN thing, when she said 'fuck off' … where there's smoke there's fire …"

Two words, spoken in a moment of frustration, followed June around for the rest of her days. And no one would have been less surprised than June to see that, in the obituaries after her death, the "fuck off incident" was inevitably cited.

All unfair. All annoying to those who knew and loved her. But maybe June has had the last laugh. It might appeal to her considerable sense of humour that after all the wonderful things she did in her life of compassionate activism and acting as a role model to at least a generation of women — and even some men — that, in the end, she might well be remembered as "The woman who said 'fuck off.'"

Well, think about it. She said "fuck off" to a lot of things in her life: injustice, unfairness, unkindness, stupidity. And yes, prejudice, in all its form.

Maybe it's not a bad epitaph after all.

Alison Gordon is a journalist and broadcaster and in the front ranks of Canadian crime fiction writers.

JOY KOGAWA ☙

ON A BUSY PRE-CHRISTMAS day, December 17, 2004, June
Callwood, Mary Jo Leddy, and I sat in Judy Sgro's constituency
office from 9:00 a.m. to 12:20 p.m. We were there because an
Eritrean man's life was in danger.

Going in and out of the office were police officers, charged
with serving and protecting Ms. Sgro's office staff from three
dangerous, trespassing women. Outside, the media waited,
seeking some sensational tidbit of news to feed hungry readers
and viewers.

We sat side by side against the window while the drama
unfolded — June in a long white coat, Mary Jo in a blue-grey
sweater over a sweater, and me in a blue Arctic parka. June's
fingers were so icy cold they were as white as her coat. Mary
Jo, the instigator of this project, sat quietly praying and planning, her eyes wide and alert. The family Mary Jo loves — the
stalwart mother whose intelligence and dignity shone in her
beautiful face, her three teenaged children, and their supporters

had been ordered outside with the media. They stood huddled under umbrellas, ready to wait for as long as necessary.

We were hungry. Especially Mary Jo. The taste of justice, so long denied, was there in her mind but tauntingly far from her grasp. All that was required was the stroke of a pen for that meal to arrive. All that was needed was to reopen a closed case of a man who had been labelled a terrorist on the basis of one interview he did not understand. He did not speak English. There had been no translator present to assist him.

The family had been separated in the chaos of the first Gulf War. Wife and children had fled, finally arriving in Toronto to live with Mary Jo at Romero house. She had grown to love them deeply. Their fidelity to their husband and father had become hers. And all feared for his safety, which had become precarious. After nine years of hoping and hassling and with all options gone, Mary Jo staged the sit-in — and the police were called.

Ms. Sgro's office staff were adamant. We had to leave. But Mary Jo was not leaving until she was assured that she could meet the minister within the next two critical days. This could not, would not, be granted. An impasse. The police and the office staff versus a handful of citizens.

At 11:45, the charming young police woman opened the waiting room door to announce that the office would be closed at noon. "Unless you leave," she said, "we'll unfortunately have to assist you out."

June, who was a personal friend of Prime Minister Paul Martin, called his office. "I'm about to be arrested," she said to his executive assistant. "I'm too old for this. My husband will be very upset with me. We only ask that Mary Jo be able to meet with the minister. It's a matter of life and death. A man's life is in danger." Within seconds a call came back from Sgro's Ottawa office — and Mary Jo was assured that the executive assistant would do everything in his power to help.

As June, Mary Jo, and I walked out peaceably into the rain and into the arms of the valiant mother of three, our tears mingled with the rain. But by late afternoon, hope had once more faded. The three children, who had travelled from the depths of anxiety over their father and soared to the heavens in hope, were plummeting again. The promise of a meeting with the minister was sent back into the bureaucracy where it languishes still.

Meanwhile, as a loving community waited and prayed, six ominous words, uttered in Judy Sgro's office, were chanted quietly in the background: "I was just doing my job." But June's parting words to one of the staff linger in the air. "A little bit of kindness goes a long way, dear," she had said, quietly, pointedly, to a woman who had denied my request to go to the bathroom. Outside, June put her white hood up in the rain, and walked on.

Joy Nozomi Kogawa is a Canadian poet and novelist of Japanese descent. Born Joy Nozomi Nakayama in Vancouver, British Columbia, she was sent to internment camps in Slocan and Coaldale, Alberta during World War II.

JOE FIORITO ～

WE LEARN BY LISTENING. I like to keep my mouth shut, and later I like to make notes:

June Callwood, in a cottage at a lake, sitting by the window telling stories. Trent Frayne, on the other side of the room, hard of hearing, napping in a chair with a book on his lap. No her without him, and vice versa.

June was talking about married life with Trent, the ups and downs. She said, "There was a time when we were both freelance, and I was selling everything, and no one was buying from him, and it was hard."

And that was long ago but we were mostly journalists in that room, and we were very quiet as we imagined how hard it would be if one person was earning and the other was not.

June said, "One night I was cleaning the fireplace at home. I had my back to him. It occurred to me that, even though I hadn't finished high school, I could go back to school and learn medicine or something. And I said that."

In other words, she would have given up her career rather than compete with him, or show him up in any way.

June paused and said, "He was silent for a time, and then he said, 'You won't make me big by making yourself small.' A man like that ..."

We were, all of us, quietly at that moment, thinking about our own marriages, and thinking about a love like that when Frayne piped up, from across the room — his hearing was acute enough at times — "Say, did you ever get the fireplace cleaned?"

She glowed. He beamed. And they went off to have a nap.

Joe Fiorito is a Toronto-based author and columnist with the Toronto Star.

MARNI JACKSON ᴐᴈ

JUNE CALLWOOD, AS WE all know, gave so many people so many things. In my case — or should I say, in my Casey — she gave me something irreplaceable: my son's name.

I knew June as a fellow journalist, and also through my long friendships with her children, Brant, Jesse, and Jill. Brant was the producer of my first ill-fated screenplay, and Jesse's big family grew up a block away from ours (our legendary music parties continue). Jill and I have worked and travelled, skied and canoed together for thirty-five years. I saw June and Trent at the odd family gathering. But I never had a chance to get to know their youngest, Casey, before he died in a motorcycle accident, at the age of twenty, in 1982.

Shortly after Casey died, I was sitting in a café on Queen Street West when I caught a glimpse of June through the front window. She was alone, dressed in white, and seemed to radiate grief. Her body was tilted forward, as if into a stiff wind. She looked like Shackleton slogging towards the South

Pole instead of a well-dressed woman strolling past the shops, and that image has stuck with me. Over the years she made it clear, in a reportorial way, how devastating it was for her to lose her younger son.

In July 1983 I gave birth to our first child, a boy. I was a freelance writer, like June (not as prolific — no one is) who had postponed motherhood 'til my late thirties. I knew nothing about babies and less than nothing about little boys. The prospect of raising one was so alarming that his father and I were stalling on the choice of a name.

About four days after he was born, Jill came to visit me in the hospital. As I was fretting about my ability to raise a son, she said something about her brother Casey, about how much pleasure June had taken from her relationship to him. What good friends they became as he grew up. "Casey," I said. "That's such a nice name."

A few days later I asked Jill whether she thought it would be all right with June if we called our son Casey. The name seemed to suit him, already, and it came with all my warm feelings for Jill and her family. But I worried that it was too soon for June to see his name float downstream to another baby. And despite her immediate blessings, I think it might have been.

Sometime during that first summer, which I remember as infernally hot, I was breast-feeding the new boy — now the king of our world — in our second-floor, un-air-conditioned kitchen. I was naked from the waist up, as I tended to be most hours of the day, an arrangement I found cooler and handier, given the round-the-clock schedule of nursing we were engaged in. The front door was unlocked downstairs. I heard someone call and then come up the steps of our apartment — the writer Sylvia Fraser, a lifelong friend of June's, wearing a pretty summer dress. "June asked me to give you this," she said, extending a present wrapped up with a bow. "She wishes she could be here as well but she's not quite up to it right now."

Neither of us remarked on my lack of clothing, which I thought was classy of Sylvia. I opened the box and found a little ceramic music box. I wound it up. Casey eyed it with interest from his latch point on the breast. It was such a bittersweet moment, to experience the shadow of June's bottomless loss at the same time that I felt my great luck as a new mother.

As it happened, Casey grew up a few blocks away from June's four grandchildren, all of whom are dear to him (he's twenty-four now) and in time both Trent and June were easily able to ask me, "How's Casey?"

My son likes his name and I can't imagine him with another. I wish I'd thought to ask June why she chose it in the first place. It's an approachable, open, friendly name, which is why it's perfect for Casey House too — it sounds like the opposite of an institution.

With June, it was always personal.

A former editor at Walrus *magazine, Marni Jackson has won numerous National Magazine Awards for her journalism. She is the author of three nonfiction books, including the bestselling memoir* The Mother Zone.

GEORGE SMITHERMAN

I GREW UP IN Islington but didn't really connect with June until 1997 when, in the megacity election, June put Barbara Hall's sign on her lawn. I was privileged to bear witness to her legacy as the provincial representative for Jessie's and Casey House. Luckier yet, she taught me masterfully that genuine moral authority, garnered by very, very few, triumphs legislative authority every time.

George Smitherman is one of Canada's leading public policy voices, having been active in public life as a grassroots organizer and community activist, and an elected official and senior advisor at the local, provincial, and federal level for more than thirty years.

Elected three times as a Member of Provincial Parliament, he served as Minister of Health and Deputy Premier of Ontario. Most recently a candidate for Toronto mayor, he has returned to his entrepreneurial roots as Chairman and Principal of G&G Global Solutions, a strategic advisory and business development boutique.

NANCY J. HARRIS

JUNE CALLWOOD CAME INTO my life only once, but she will remain in my heart forever.

I began working in a newly opened women's shelter in Southern Ontario in the early 1980s. Women helping women and their children, staff pulling together to make a safe, loving environment. They, along with the volunteers, became the backbone of all aspects of that successful shelter's life.

About eight years after the formation of this shelter that had provided a new beginning for hundreds of women and children, something began to go terribly wrong. Occupancy rates dropped dramatically and, as a result, funding was sharply reduced. Blame was placed on the counselling staff without any justification.

The staff knew that the cause of the problems stemmed from issues unrelated to the counselling provided but, when they went to the board members with their concerns, they were ignored. As the only staff member who was not dependent on my position for my livelihood, and out of sheer desperation that the shelter would close, I wrote an honest, factual letter outlining the obvious problems that existed. Within two weeks, I was fired without cause.

I was devastated at this injustice. Then an article appeared in a Toronto newspaper questioning June Callwood's work in a shelter. Her plight sounded so much like mine that I wrote a consoling letter to her, never expecting a reply.

In the weeks following my writing to June, and in part based on my letter to the shelter board, others got involved and investigations confirmed my concerns. Then, a letter arrived that put what she and I had both experienced into perspective. June's words of wisdom helped me to move on. With encouragement such as she provided, along with that of professionals with whom I had worked at the shelter, I opened my own counselling practice. Over the next twenty years I saw hundreds of women, first here in Ontario and then in British Columbia.

Because of June Callwood's fairness, caring, and passion for women's work, I was able to continue to assist in giving abused women a voice. Thank you June Callwood. You are my hero!

Nancy J. Harris was born and raised in Brantford, Ontario and worked for several years as a nurse at the Oakville Trafalgar Memorial Hospital. She later worked at the Nova Vita Women's Shelter in Brantford, first as the volunteer coordinator and then as a counsellor. Subsequently, she started her own private practice providing counselling services to clients in Brantford and

Fenwick, Ontario before moving to British Columbia. Now back in Ontario, Nancy is involved with running groups that support women in a church setting on a pro bono basis in Fonthill.

CHARLES PACHTER ❧

I GOT TO KNOW June personally in the late 1970s when the Writers' Development Trust rented offices in my Artists' Alliance Building at 24 Ryerson Avenue. June drove around in a sporty little convertible that she delighted in. One day I found her, dressed in miniskirt and slingback heels, on her way to yet another fundraiser, fretting in the parking lot over a flat tire, so I came over to help her change it. I was no mechanic but managed to help the damsel in distress. I jacked the car up, unscrewed the bolts to remove the flat, and mounted the spare as June chatted to me about her projects. She was so impressed that she went around describing my tire-changing prowess to everyone we met at parties for the next few years. That was my hook with June until she bought one of my Canadian flag silkscreen prints and boasted to everyone she was a major Pachter collector.

In the early eighties, after I was downed by the recession and lost all my real estate holdings in the Queen Street West area, June decided to interview me for her *National Treasures* TV series. She seemed fascinated that, as an artist, I had not jumped off a bridge, that I had made a comeback, and moved on from my Ten Loft Years of renovating old dumps. One of her more stringent observations in the interview was her inability to comprehend how I, being so sociable and gregarious, came home to an empty house. Her wonderful long-term relationship with husband Trent Frayne obviously coloured her observation. When I told her that living alone for me had always seemed perfectly natural, that for some artists it was essential, she was stymied, offering her opinion that I didn't know what I was missing. For a brief time she made me feel inadequate, but I got over it.

Charles Pachter is a Toronto painter, printmaker, designer, historian, and lecturer, and an Officer of the Order of Canada.

VAL ROSS ❧

1968. MY USUALLY SKEPTICAL mother fell in love with June
Callwood around the time June's picture was plastered on
newspaper front pages (the cops were hauling June away
because she had been protesting their treatment of hippies).
My mum always liked underdogs. She sensed that June did
too, and for her sympathies was being oppressed by those with
power. Yet I saw June as an overdog: great clothes, fabulous
journalistic skills, witty friends, and a snazzy sports car. (Once,
when I went to a party with June's son Barney, he took me
for a spin in it.) Above all she had real power, because she
was such an articulate moral force. In most people, righteousness is annoying. In June, it flamed out gorgeously — like an
abstract painting by Gershon Iskowitz that she had hanging
in her house, radiant in sunny yellow, orange, and apricot.
Barney said, if memory serves, something about it not being
easy being the son of a saint.

Luckily, Saint June was blessed with a sense of humour

and self-awareness. Once I asked her about her contretemps with Robertson Davies, whom she had interviewed for *Maclean's* magazine in 1952. At the time, she thought him hostile and contemptuous. I suggested that perhaps Davies, a shy man, was afraid of her and of her nosing around his life. June looked surprised. Then she recalled that when she'd gone to see Davies she was making a name for herself writing exposés like the one about a comedy troupe known as the Happy Gang. ("They thought I was there to be their publicist and they all told me how they hated one another," she laughed, "so I wrote about the Unhappy Gang.") So yes, June admitted cheerfully, she was a toughie even back then. "Davies was right to be worried about me. Come to think of it, I was a pain in the ass."

Val Ross was an arts reporter for The Globe and Mail *and the author of two children's books,* The Road to There *and* You Can't Read This. *Her book* Robertson Davies: A Portrait in Mosaic *was published shortly after her death in 2008.*

WALTER PITMAN

MY MEMORY OF JUNE relates to her enormous courage.

When the federal government inflicted the War Measures Act on the Province of Quebec, June was very active in the Canadian Civil Liberties Association. Needless to say, the CCLA opposed the action, refusing to believe the government of the province was about to collapse. June became a spokesperson — for a very unpopular cause.

June faced angry and outraged people — many of whom were her friends. Her work on behalf of young unmarried mothers, youth, and children may have brought her accolades and support, but this issue brought her only humiliation and defeat.

She never backed down for a second ... even though she was risking her reputation and her employment. She even stiffened the resolve of many males who were facing the same reaction. She was fearless when she knew she was right.

Walter Pitman is a Toronto teacher, journalist, administrator, and author. Although his last years with June were associated with the Campaign Against Child Poverty, he also remembers that she was a bulwark with the Canadian Civil Liberties Association. June was named an Honorary Life Director of the CCLA in 1988.

MOLLY JOHNSON ⌒

NOT EVER HAVING HAD a driver's licence, and always (well almost always) managing without one — you know, that *relying on the kindness of strangers and my husband* thing — left me always a little more in awe of the obviously awesome June. She would swing onto our tiny downtown street in her Miata and park in our no-parking lane (where she inevitably got a ticket, yet somehow never seemed to care — kind of a "fuck you" thing). We would then pile into that sports car, cruising top-down through Chinatown on Spadina heading to Queen, and downtown we flew. It represented all that June, and only June, had in the same package: courage, freedom, speed, smarts, style, forgiveness, respect. That's what June taught me. From behind the wheel of her car.

Molly Johnson lives near Kensington Market and is still thinking about getting her licence — amongst other things that June inspired.

J. ROSS ROBINSON

THE ANGLICAN FUNERAL SERVICE is often a stubborn piece of work. To a clear-eyed nonbeliever like June Callwood, her dear friend's autopsy report was going to hold greater promise.

June and Stoney joked that they would spend their old age together as full blown eccentrics in red wigs, drinking sherry. June and Stoney were both shy of fifty when Stoney died. They shared an apartment in Toronto early in World War II, before either was married, and remained close thereafter.

First, June married Trent. Then Stoney (whose real name was Marion, but was nicknamed "Stonewall" for her last name, Jackson) married a man too self-righteous for her mixture of mischief and sorrow. For years, June met Stoney's train at Union Station when Stoney ran away from home. She displaced either Jill or Jesse whenever she decamped Montreal for a room at the Fraynes. June spoke to Stoney's shrinks. She sent her to job interviews that held little reality and to divorce lawyers who might stick with her.

The day of Stoney's funeral is best remembered for its icy back roads, a veil of early January freezing rain and the Anglican minister who officiated. He wore his overshoes under his white surplus, facing the small group of mourners in the drab, shuttered, and utterly unremarkable country funeral parlour. He walked to the front beside the casket without a word or nod of recognition to Stoney's daughter and son in the front pew.

The minister was young and tightly wound with determination. He wore boys' brown snow boots with long straps that snaffled his pant legs tight at mid-calf. Had he carried a saddlebag you'd have pegged him as a circuit riding missionary and prayed for his horse.

June winced when the young man choked out the name of the departed: "Mary." Stoney's Christian name was Marian. With penitential calm he declared, "We die because we have sinned." June looked over at Stoney's ninety-five-year-old father on the arm of his nurse. A man of dignity and wit, this was the final blow. Now he had outlived three of his children — two boys with RCAF wings, both friends to June, had been killed in the war. Frail and old, he had given Stoney sanctuary in his house in the Caledon Hills these last years. If he bought her a new car and it ended up in the ditch like the others, it was a test of his mercy.

Near the end of the service, his eyes fixed on the far wall, the young minister raised a question of religious doubt. He was uncertain, he said, but he believed that God could love those who had messed up their lives.

Tread softly, Reverend, in those oversized boots, for you have tread on June's dream of growing old and eccentric with her friend.

June tracked the minister down on the steps of the funeral home. This sainted woman was not gentle of tongue when she said clearly to his face: "You are a pompous, insensitive asshole."

Ross Robinson lives in Creemore, Ontario, where he raises Highland cattle and writes plays for the regional theatre.

JOSEPH WONG ∽

JUNE WAS ABLE TO bring people with different points of views together. The fact that she founded or co-founded over fifty social action organizations speaks volumes about her commitment to social equality, her boundless energy, and her concern for other people's pain.

As a visible minority and immigrant to Canada and having experienced the anguish of racism myself, June gave me hope that racism is not an invincible social reality — that it can be confronted and defeated. As a white woman, she bravely challenged racist practices by helping minority groups who face systemic racism and by speaking in support for those who have been unfairly targeted as scapegoats in society. Her courageous challenges to power and racist ideologies, I think, served as proof of her steely determination and tenacious spirit. What I came to know about June was that once she declared her devotion to a cause, she would not back down, she could not — it was simply not in her nature.

June Callwood was instrumental in the founding of the Harmony Movement when she came out and supported the nascent organization in a defining race-relations issue in the City of Markham. As honorary patron, she actively championed many of the organization's causes. In 2004, the Harmony Movement awarded her its Harmony Award and named their scholarship program after her. The 2007 award was given to Casey House in June's honour.

Dr. Joseph Wong is Harmony Movement's founding co-chair.

LINDA RAPSON ⌒

Wednesday, March 28, 2007

GREAT NEWS FOR YOU all: June is comfortable, cozy, her funny self and not in pain. Yesterday was a bit tough very briefly, but these palliative care docs know what to do and all is well. She is not overly sedated, so her mind is as sharp as ever, she can snooze off whenever she feels like it and she can enjoy her family and the growing floral display.

Tonight I had the best visit we've had yet. I showed up after work and found her awake in the semi-darkness, as cheery as could be. I wasn't going to stay very long, but she declared that she was very cozy and really loves the bed; the pillows were somehow arranged just exactly right so that she really looked comfortable and we had a chat full of laughter. She told me about the family visits of the day. Her sister Jane and her husband and nephew arrived from Texas. Granddaughter Bree, June's guy "Trent-Call-Me-Bill," son Brant (aka Barney), Jill, Jesse, etc. all were there. She liked the idea that granddaughter Marie and her boyfriend Justin sat in the hall and did their "homework" today and we old fogies marvelled at the thought that Marie can actually write exams at McGill online from here! She's in engineering, can you imagine? Amazing.

And Marie's sweet sister Emma is here after returning to the city from a stint up north for a course she is doing. I'm not sure whether Lucy, her youngest granddaughter, a don at Victoria College, was there today, but she's been there a lot. That leaves gorgeous Jack Manchester, little brother to Marie, Emma, and Lucy, who was there yesterday. He's a student at Vic and is in the same residence where Lucy is a don. Neat, eh?

In the course of our conversation tonight June said that it was really fortuitous that I had arrived, since she had been lying there wondering how to turn off the bathroom light that was shining in her eyes, and I was the lucky person who was going to do it for her. You see, when you are an Independent Woman, you must never, ever ring for the nurse! It is forbidden. The prospect of trying to do it herself and falling on the floor deterred her, since then the nurses would be mad at her.

That done, I read her a bit from some of the notes I've received, mainly the funny bits. She howled with laughter when I quoted Jay MacGillivray as saying, "ya might wanna stop calling her "the great lady" — makes her sound like a great lakes freighter." She was ever so pleased that Jim Bratton is becoming a grandfather this week and told me what a wonderful family he has. Alison Gordon's report that she had dreamed about June went over big, since Alison said, "It was a happy dream, full of champagne and music, with you at the centre of it, telling everyone what to do!" It wasn't just June who appreciated Shelley Ambrose's remark, "And hugs and kisses and love to her and to Trent (sexiest man in Canada)." I personally informed T-C-M-B about his status later this evening. For an eighty-eight-year-old, he took it very calmly.

June and I each had an organic banana from the bunch on her table, which she declared was absolutely delicious (it was), and off I went, feeling uplifted and happy.

Thanks for the messages you have sent. I hope you read Theresa Dobko's excellent contribution yesterday. Some of the messages from people are really sweet, like this from Denise Donlon: "Am sending our best and warmest wishes and prayers to June. I worked with her and Molly on Kumbaya and have many wonderful memories of her and pastries, sunshine, laughter, hard work, great legs, feisty determination and the most divine of inspiration." And from Sally Armstrong: "I cannot imagine not having June to guide, push, reassure and challenge me and everyone else."

Truth be told, I think there's a book here somewhere, just of quotes. And I haven't shared with you all the passionately emotional statements of love and concern, admiration and wonder at the influence that this woman has had on all of us. I have, however, printed them all and taken them to her room, hoping that she will pick them up to read or someone will read them to her.

Now, a word about someone you haven't heard enough about. Cheryl Wagner, June's family physician (and mine) is truly a wonder and an inspiration. She has been totally attentive to June for these many years. She keeps in touch with the specialists, advocates when necessary even if she has to spend endless time on the telephone, makes house calls, appears early in the morning at the hospital and just cares so much. She and I have been calling each other after every visit so we both know exactly what is going on and have had many a late night chat that usually ends up with us sharing our favourite anecdotes about this remarkable journey. Cheryl is a McMaster grad. They were taught to problem solve, starting with the first classes over thirty years ago. And she is a pro at it. If she doesn't know something, she finds out about it. She takes time to listen and she examines her patients. Those of you who are doctor-less will, however, have to stop thinking that you would like to sign on with Cheryl, because she is all booked up. It was June's lucky day when I switched to Cheryl and June followed. We have the same dentist too.

Then there is the Great Man himself, Professor S. Lawrence Librach — W. Gifford-Jones Professor, Pain Control & Palliative Care, University of Toronto and Director, Temmy Latner Centre for Palliative Care, Mount Sinai Hospital — or "Larry," as we like to call him. He agreed in January to be June's palliative care doc but happened to be out of the country when she was admitted. He is now back and was a welcome sight this morning. In his absence and on an ongoing basis, June is in the very capable hands of Dr. Giovanna Sirianni. She and the wonderful nurses at the PMH Palliative Care Unit have made her as comfortable as she can be and June appreciates them all.

Now I must say a word about the remarkable other member of our medical team, Dr. Shirley Douglas. You may not recognize who that is right away, but if I give you a hint that the Dr. title is honorary, bestowed and supported by the patient and Dr. Wagner, you may recognize her as the undisputed saviour of medicare in Canada. I have known Shirley a little for many years, probably close to thirty, but I never appreciated what a strong, funny, sensible, and warm woman she is until this past week. She is such a comfort to me and to Cheryl, and to June's family. Thanks, Shirley, for everything. Having said that, I can't resist sharing the following conversation I had with her last week, since she may never see this: I (I was going to say "Me," then remembered that Callwood will come back from the grave to correct my English): "Shirley, do you have an email address?" Shirley: "No." I: "Do you have a fax machine?" Shirley: (I swear this is true) "It's out of ink." So Dr. Shirley is email-less and will only see this if one of you (maybe Rachel Sutherland?) PRINTS it and gives it to her, or I print it and snail mail it to her. Bet she doesn't know what "snail mail" means!

I hope that you share my joy in knowing our friend June (Joon?) is as ready to go and as content with her circumstances as anyone could be under these conditions. Few of

us have seen anyone face death this way. It is an inspiration.
Here's to June.

With love to all,
Linda

*Linda Rapson was one of June's closest friends. She is a physician
and was one of the founders of Casey House Hospice.*

JOEY SLINGER ❧

WHEN YOU BUY A plant with one of those tags saying "full sun," "full sun" doesn't necessarily mean *full* sun.

When you buy a plant that promises to flourish in "full shade," "full shade" doesn't necessarily mean *full* shade.

Today, these and other astounding things your gardening correspondent has learned the hard way.

This isn't going to be a gardening column, is it?

I'm afraid so.

Every now and then my garden gets an idea into its head, and when it does I find the best thing to do is go with it. (Like I have any say in the matter.) This spring the idea was lupine. Note the singular.

For a good ten years, the idea in my head had also been lupine — actually lupines; when I get an idea it's grandiose — and planted lots. And every spring a few leaves would emerge. Then disappear. Forever.

I did not accidentally pull them out. I didn't because my

wife would always point out the new shoots and say, "Those are lupines. If you pull them out, I will break your knees."

So for the last couple of years I haven't planted any. (I know when I'm whipped.) And this year — spang! — one shot up. Immense. Eight lavender-blue flower spikes already. You might think this is ironic. Not me. I think my garden is telling me where we stand in relation to one another. It's giving me the finger.

Peonies like full sun.

No they don't. Not if they're against a south-facing board fence where, in this season, they get more intense sunlight than cactuses in the Mojave Desert. Bloom one day. Take your breath away. Next day the flowers are crisp and brown as a handful of Pringles. Aw, c'mon!

I know "full shade" doesn't mean like under the car, but I've tried every conceivable "full shade" plant to cover an embarrassing patch under the lilacs. Nothing works. So forget it. Stop punishing yourself. I know that's ridiculous advice to give a gardener, and maybe someday I'll take it. The plain fact is that what you end up with in full shade is what you got the "full shade" plants to cover: dirt.

Twenty-three years ago, when we started this garden — the first either of us had ever attempted — June Callwood showed up with a garden-warming gift. "You'll find," she said, presenting us with a rhododendron, about knee-high, in a pot, "this plant will be the work of a lifetime."

And she laughed.

And we laughed.

And after a couple of years — including winters (rhododendrons are on your case about something or other every single month) — I finally got that son of a bitch to bloom. A couple of blooms anyway. But enough for me to declare myself "Rhodo King of Riverdale." June Callwood; what did she know?

I got more rhodos. Lots more. I had the touch. And over the years I've managed to get some of them to bloom too. A bit. Sometimes. And by eating on the run, I have enough time left to catch a little sleep.

One spring, when she was becoming really ill, June's rhodo did something strange and magnificent, flowering like it never had before: a raging pink bonfire in the corner where it had stood since she gave it to us.

Then over the summer it began to fail. Nothing I did made any difference. By the time winter came, the leaves, far from evergreen, were black. The day June died, I dug it out, dead, too, in root and branch. Its glory left to memory alone.

Joey Slinger wrote this column in the Toronto Star. *He was a long-standing friend of June Callwood.*

MARJORIE HARRIS ~

I MET JUNE CALLWOOD back in the early 1960s when she and her husband, Trent Frayne, came to an opening at the art gallery where I worked. Like a couple of movie stars, June and Bill (that's how he is known to his friends) were so jaw-droppingly gorgeous that they almost glowed. June was going through what she called her nursery-colour period — all pinks, yellows, and blues — and I gave her the name of the store where I shopped ("How about a little black?") and we yakked on about clothes.

Over the years, we talked about everything at one time or another, from babies to death and back again. There was no subject she wouldn't tackle in a way that was at once serious and merry. June was a sassy girl. She flirted with fellows right up to her last interview with CBC-TV host George Stroum-boulopoulos two weeks before she died.

I remember June best from the 2005 Lakefield Literary Festival in Ontario, which celebrates the birthday of novelist and friend Margaret Laurence. We were all staying at journalists Elizabeth and John Gray's wonderful old cottage on the lake — ten writers and journalists of one sort or another. But there was an old-time camaraderie between us all that only years and years of contact can put together.

June and Bill arrived in her Miata. "He's been nagging at me since I pulled out of the garage," she announced gaily when they came in. Her guy — as she called Bill — and "your guy," as she called my husband, Jack Batten, wandered off to a corner to swap anecdotes. These men do not go to parties without checking what time the other is arriving. June got so she'd call first and ask, "What time will you get your guy there?" These men like to sit; they especially like to sit in kitchens and they like to be able to hear each other. Once Bill was settled, June would spin off all around, making each person feel like every minute she had was for them.

Hard to believe when looking at this serene woman what a wretched childhood she had — poverty and an absent father in small-town Belle River, Ontario, near Windsor, or that life's tragedies had not left a horrific visual mark on her. The youngest of her four kids, Casey, was killed by a drunk driver in 1982; she never recovered from it. Her second oldest, Barney, became wheelchair-bound after brain surgery gone wrong. If you didn't know, you couldn't tell.

We knew June as a writer, endlessly inventive, always bang-on about a new and tragic disease or social eruption. AIDS was one of fifty causes she espoused. And she founded

Casey House, Canada's first hospice for victims of the disease.

She was a terrific author, and produced riveting work: thirty books and 1,500 newspaper and magazine articles, including a monthly *Chatelaine* column in the 1950s, ghostwritten for Toronto obstetrician Dr. Marion Hilliard. The most famous was a 1956 piece on a woman's right to sexual pleasure — instantly selling out on newsstands. The column led to a bestselling book, *A Woman Doctor Looks at Life and Love*, which in turn led to June's flourishing career as a major ghostwriter (creating popular memoirs for filmmaker Otto Preminger, broadcaster Barbara Walters, and labour leader Bob White).

But it was June's own byline that became a household name. And though she was prolific and well-read, she never found writing easy and always let other journalists know when she admired what they did. She knew just what was involved all too well.

At the cottage, we sat sipping tea for a few hours, nattering away, and my memory of her will always be just how lovely her skin looked in that afternoon light. There was no vanity anymore. Wrinkles really didn't matter, only people. And if she needed a new outfit, she'd just reach farther back into the closet until she was wearing things we'd all seen decades before when this sort of thing might have been more important to her.

Several years ago, when the Grays first tooled around Lakefield, Ontario (population 2,199), with June and Bill in tow, it was, in Elizabeth's words, electrifying to see people stop, stare, then cross the street to say hello to June. When she went to a friend's exhibition, they crowded into the local art gallery just because they needed to speak to her.

We had one of those unforgettable cottage dinners: endless talk and laughter. Boy, did we laugh. No one mentioned that June had terminal cancer. What we talked about was some unsuspecting politician she'd tackled, or maybe it was how to divide up the five desserts she'd brought.

This was a typical June thing: generosity. Right up until the last week, when she was clapped into hospital for the last time, she accepted invitations — "What shall I bring? Champagne? Dessert?" — always saying she didn't want to miss this party because it would be full of her favourite people.

She made us all feel that way. Her friend and doctor, Linda Rapson, who kept everyone in touch with June until that day in April when she died, describes June as someone who nurtured friendships like a loving gardener: she kept them alive and helped them grow. She was fiercely loyal, honest to a fault, witty, and full of both wisdom and perspective.

Oh my, how true. After her death, it wasn't until we gathered at the next party — at the Grays, of course — and there was no June taking up a space in the front hall with a kiss, a hug and a word of cheer, that the reality of her absence hit.

Pace June. What a hole you have left behind.

Marjorie Harris is editor-at-large of Gardening Life *and a garden columnist for* The Globe and Mail. *Her new book,* How to Make a Garden: The 7 Essential Steps for Canadian Gardeners, *has been published by Random House.*

CHARLOTTE STEIN ⁓

I MET JUNE AT a Booksellers Association Conference where I asked her to sign my copy of *Twelve Weeks in Spring*. At the time, my mother was recovering from breast cancer and we talked about that. June was extremely lovely and wrote a beautiful salutation in a copy of the book that I gave to my mother.

Years later I was at Variety Village with my son, who uses a wheelchair. He was there doing some sports. When I saw June coming out, she was pushing the wheelchair of her son, Barney. I didn't speak to her — I always feel that someone who is a "celebrity" deserves her privacy — but I knew that her son Casey had died and that we all experience the same grief when an adult child dies.

I know June's daughter, Jill, slightly. I like her very much. When she came into my store and told me her mother was ill and expected to die soon, I wrote to June, saying how much I had always admired her and that her life had mattered to me as I had followed her in the news with admiration and respect. She wrote a lovely letter in reply — just proving that, even then, she was still being kind to others.

I admired her determination to live life to its fullest, in spite of heartbreaking experiences. Like June, I was determined that the death of one son and the disability of the other would not ruin my pleasure in life, and June proved it could be done — this all apart from her great work and goodness for so many others.

Charlotte Stein is the owner of a bookstore in Parry Sound.

MICHAEL ENRIGHT ⁓

I MET JUNE CALLWOOD one warm evening in the summer of 1961 at a racetrack. She was as beautiful as blazes and newly pregnant with Casey. I was working for her husband, the glorious Trent Frayne, in the public relations office of Old Woodbine racetrack (later renamed Greenwood, and now the site of a cheesy subdivision that looks like Happyville, USA).

June would drive from the farthest reaches of Etobicoke to the east end of Toronto to have supper in the racetrack dining room with her fella.

Hormonal eighteen-year-olds aren't usually smitten by older women — they're too much like your mother. But Callwood's beauty was stunningly luminescent; she could literally stop your breath for a few seconds. And she had style; dressed to kill, she seemed to float on some hidden pillar of air.

At the end of that summer's race meeting, we parted company; I went back to school for a while and later got a job on a small town newspaper.

June had taken to calling me Holden. For some reason I reminded her of Holden Caulfield, the anti-hero of *The Catcher in the Rye*. From that moment, I was Holden forever.

I later moved to England and lost touch with June and Bill [Trent]. When I returned to Canada, I got married and started to raise a family. When our first son was born, June was there to give plenty of advice about parenting, about being a father. "It's never easy, Holden," she said, "but it's the most important thing you'll ever do."

Over the years we would meet occasionally at Brown's, her favourite lunch restaurant, to gossip, exchange rumours, talk about children and causes. The one topic we never talked about was my love for riding motorcycles. Casey was killed in 1982 when a drunk driver hit his motorcycle. June never fully recovered. In the ensuing years, I never rode my bike to her Hillcroft home.

When she was diagnosed with her various cancers, she seemed to be more concerned about her friends than herself. "Holden, it's not a big deal."

During the course of her illness and treatment we would meet for lunch less frequently. The last time was about a week before she entered Princess Margaret Hospital. She swept into the restaurant, magnificently turned out as usual and, as usual, customers stopped eating to stare at her. We gossiped for a while, ordered, ate, played with our wine. In the middle of lunch my cellphone rang. It was my oldest son, Daniel. June grabbed the phone and proceeded to tell him which condoms worked and which didn't. She wanted him to be careful.

Then she turned serious. "Holden, I want you to do something for me; it's really important." Knowing as we both did that this would be the last time we had lunch together, I tried to match her sombre tone.

"Of course, June, anything."

"I want you to tell people, nicely, to stop bringing me squash soup. Every time I turn around, there is somebody with a bowl of squash soup. Tell, me, Holden, is it supposed to be the soup of the dying?"

She died peacefully two weeks later.

It is still hard to believe that June Callwood is gone, but she is.

And so, I'm afraid, is Holden.

Michael Enright is host of The Sunday Edition — CBC *Radio's national Sunday morning program.*

EMILY HEARN ⟨∽

I FISHED INTO AN old chest in my bedroom where diaries are
kept; diaries that go back to the beginning of time — mine
and June's time, that is. We have both lived eighty-two years
and these diaries record our girlhood together in a Kitchener
high school where as a gabby, lively, younger-than-the-others
pair we spent time together in and out of class, wandering
about our small town, swimming in the public pool where I
admired her beautiful diving, being way too timid myself to go
up on the high board which she fearlessly climbed and sprang
from with effortless grace. She was born to challenge.

After she moved to Regina, then Brantford, we led surpris-
ingly parallel professional and personal lives, marrying early,
each having four children, each losing a beloved son, each
writing for a living. There our paths differed, she becoming
the powerful journalist whose words influenced us all and I
choosing children's media and poetry. We were schooled by
the same brilliant teacher, Kenneth Millar, a Coleridge scholar

who later changed his name and became the renowned detective-writer, Ross MacDonald. Even then he valued our talents, tried to help June get to university, which circumstances in her life prevented. She didn't need it to achieve her gifted potential.

We shared our last hug at the meeting where young Evie Freedman disputed so eloquently the projected banning of Deborah Ellis's *Three Wishes*. In her last note to me in 2006, when I sent her my first adult poetry collection, we agreed that we had all we wanted in life, to have loved and been loved. "On we go, dear friend," she wrote.

I don't "miss" her — she is inside me, as she has been from first feeling the impact of her vivacity, style, instant response and deep kindness.

Emily Hearn is a poet, scriptwriter of children's programs for CBC *and* TVO, *and writer of children's books for Second Story Press. She wrote "Mighty Mites" for* Owl Magazine *with artist Mark Thurman and is an ongoing mentor of children's creative writing online.*

NANCY GRAHAM ·⊙~

IT WAS A BLUSTERY, bone-chilling March afternoon in 1996 when I first met June Callwood. We'd both braved the elements from our respective Etobicoke homes up to the northern reaches of the city for our first "mentor-mentoree" rendezvous as part of the Toronto Public Library Writer-in-Residence Program. June was suffering from a nasty cold and I was trembling from nerves: it's not everyday one has the privilege of being in the company of a Companion of the Order of Canada, whose achievements as an author, journalist, and social activist are legendary. I kept passing June Kleenexes. June being June, she put me at such ease with her warmth and gentle, self-effacing manner that I quickly lapsed into a bewildering comfort zone.

"You are a writer," she assured me that day, an echo I continue to hear during my lowest writing ebbs. The book June mentored me through was about depression and her candour about her own experiences with the great leveller was never lost on me. "You wrote me such a wonderful letter that

I'm going to hang on to it forever as a bulwark against the blues," she once typed on her trademark cream stationery.

As one of the many souls who entered June's expansive circle of light (and her Miatas!), I was gifted with an extraordinary friendship nestled largely in correspondence and coffee, flowers and fruit baskets — the latter two of which I had a penchant for sending June every few months. Just because.

In April 2005 I became the proud owner of "June's Broom," a sturdy six-string corn broom up for auction at the annual Joy Kogawa–inspired Toronto Dollar Event. A veritable life talisman (never to touch a floor!), it is mounted alongside a "Certificate of Authenticity" that reads:

> Sweeping Clean ... Please use this broom to sweep away the evils Gandhi described as "untruth, injustice, and humbug." When that is done, sweep in kindness, beauty and decency. Don't give up.

June, of course, was the epitome of kindness. And determination. In her January 2007 letter, June wrote, "I'm in a bad patch with cancer right now, but I will be springing up soon and we'll toast survival with large cups of coffee." In our case, those large cups of coffee were usually consumed at her favourite Second Cup at Royal York and Bloor, "because moms and toddlers use it as a drop-in centre mid-mornings, and babies always cheer me up a lot."

On the afternoon of March 14, 2007, another equally positive note popped up on my computer: "The roses are still opening, and they are the size of lions' paws. Everyone stops to stare and smell them, especially me. What a stunning gift. I have plenty of time to enjoy them because I am housebound with all the stuff my cancer is causing. Friday I go to St. Mike's for something that might help me breath, a rather good idea, and after that you and I should dance around the May pole. I am so very, very grateful for your kindness. Love, June."

Oh, dear June, no amount of kindness was enough ...

Nancy Graham is a writer and the author of Afraid of the Day: A Daughter's Journey *(Women's Press 2003). She has held positions in both the non-profit and community services sectors, and for many years, has been involved with the Jean Tweed Centre, a forerunner in the field of substance abuse treatment programs for women and their families. She is currently employed by the Toronto Public Library.*

ARTHUR BIELFELD ✒

THE LAST TIME I sent flowers to June Callwood for her birthday was December 2, 2006. Her real birthday was June 2, but that was an occasion she doubted would take place, so we observed the halfway mark. We had met for lunch the day before at one of my favourite haunts. Our waitress thought she recognized June and asked, "Are you the Rabbi's wife?" June chuckled and replied, somewhat cryptically, "Even better!" To which the perplexed server responded testily, "What then, his mistress?" At that moment I didn't know where to put myself, but June thought it was hilarious. Over the years that delicious sense of humour often softened her own pain and gave perspective to the pain she saw around her.

June was one of the kindest human beings I have ever known. Some time ago she involved me in an organization that never did make it off the ground. Midway through one interminable meeting June looked at her watch, jumped up, and exclaimed, "My goodness! I have to go visit my prostitutes!"

and she disappeared out the door. Her compassion seemed to extend to every marginalized group and every suffering human being.

She was invariably honest. If she disagreed with someone's point of view, she managed to present her own opinions with lucidity and charm, but never with an edginess that might embarrass the other person. She was an extraordinary listener, sympathetic without being false, able to hear beyond the surface chatter until she honed in on the issues of the heart. And then, in a few well-chosen words, she would offer a response, or simply by her silence make you feel that you had the undivided attention of someone who cared deeply about you.

Yet, beneath her soft textured surface, there was a tempered core. June was passionate about those things that mattered most to her. Whether as a writer, a civil libertarian or a social activist, she was willing to get down and dirty in order to achieve her goals. On at least two occasions I heard our former prime minister admit that he was afraid of June. I don't believe that Paul Martin was just trying to be affable. He recognized her moral authority and relentless zeal in pursuing her vision.

Two days before she died we had our last conversation. She was barely able to speak more than a few sentences. As I leaned over her hospital bedrail to catch her words, she fell asleep holding my hands. A few minutes later, her granddaughter, Emma, walked into the room. June opened her eyes and in a clear voice said, "Arthur, I had a dream about you. I was in a parking lot with the gate closed. You came and unlocked the gate so that the children could come in and the old people could leave." These were the last words I heard her speak. June was ready to leave this world to make room for the birth of new life — her beloved children.

Happy birthday, June.

Arthur Bielfeld is Rabbi Emeritus of Temple Emanu-El and co-chair of the Campaign Against Child Poverty.

PAM McCONNELL ⟋

DEAREST JUNE,

It's Thanksgiving weekend. Jim and I are in Ottawa celebrating our fortieth anniversary, surrounded by family, fun, and love. All weekend I've been missing you — and giving thanks for you.

In 1984, I was a wide-eyed new trustee with the Toronto Board of Education, ready to tackle child poverty on my first visit to City Hall. I walked into committee room 4, for the Children's Network meeting you co-chaired. There you were, chatting with Dorothy Thomas about your families, politics, and kids. Even before that moment, your books, interviews, and the stories about you had helped shape my focus. I was thankful to spend that meeting studying your every move, word, and idea. You weren't holding court. You focused on battles to be won — forming strategies, recruiting soldiers, and presenting marching orders.

I am thankful that you showed us that it was the act, not

the actors, that mattered. You capitalized on our strengths and experiences and pushed us to exceed beyond our own expectations. We crafted children's surveys, council motions, vision statements, and funding requests to make a real difference for children.

I am thankful that you showed us how to turn idealism into action. You sent me to the director of education for funding for the children's safety manual. It was the first time I had to ask for funding (and I'm sure you had a quiet word with the director to ensure that I succeeded and would have the confidence to ask again — and ask for more).

I am thankful that you always asked for more, and made sure I asked for more from myself. I continued to learn as we worked together in Women Against Amalgamation. When I ran against former allies for a seat on the amalgamated city council, you were there to give me the strength and confidence to understand that, in the council chamber, it was my responsibility to be a voice for women.

I am thankful for our victories — the Children's Report Card, the Children's Summit, the Davenport Perth Neighbourhood Centre, and the Children's Charter that was embedded into the city's official plan. I am also thankful for the setbacks — for being together on St. James Cathedral's steps, the bells tolling on the government-declared date for the end of child poverty. You refused to quit.

The last time I saw you was when we named the laneway after you. I am thankful for that image of you basking in the sun, and smiling at the children as you talked with the young mothers. You taught me to continue that legacy — not only in the act, but in the nurturing of others to continue the fight.

I am giving thanks for everything you have been in my life — for your voice, your smile, and your wisdom. I wish you were here. But you are here in every wish that becomes realized. You are here in the children's laughter and their mothers' joy.

Love and thanks,

Pam

Pam McConnell is a councillor for the City of Toronto. She served as Vice-Chair of the Toronto Police Services Board from 2003–2010, including serving as Chair in 2004, and has also been an advocate of children's issues on city council.

PAT CAPPONI ⌒

I'D NEVER SAY THIS if she were still alive — she'd be very annoyed. Throughout our relationship, I had to work hard to hide my admiration, that sense of being struck with awe of the woman every time we were together. She'd be merciless if she suspected I was not seeing her as she was — if I looked at her through the eyes of a fan, not a friend.

Not that she didn't like adulation — she clearly did — but from her friends she expected a more realistic appraisal of who and what she was.

So, June, if you're reading this, I apologize, but truly, I always viewed our friendship as one of those acts of kindness that was second nature to you. How else to explain it? We met at the wake of Margaret Frazer, and again when she came to the drop-in to interview me for *Twelve Weeks in Spring*, and during that interview came about a mutual and lasting recognition of the grief we both bore, a grief buried under actions and a carefully constructed public persona. We became immediate friends, the hat-wearing, cigarette-smoking, psychiatric survivor activist and the incomparable June.

The thing with June was, it wasn't all one-sided, so that you felt diminished in any way, as if you'd encountered a Lady Bountiful doing charitable works. She'd tell you if she was worried or upset, about her family or friends or some public furor, she had an intrinsic understanding that by her accepting advise and comfort she made it easier to be her friend rather than an acolyte. We'd talk of death and dying, of being life weary at times, and though she'd never been suicidal, she declared that, if she happened to be standing at the edge of a cliff, she wouldn't mind if someone gave her a push.

It was June who started me on my writing career, telling me I was good enough, getting me an agent, and ensuring my first manuscript got noticed by Penguin. She even came up with the title. And when she heard from mutual friends that I didn't have a stove in my room, she buzzed up in her little sports car — a huge box sticking out of the trunk — and happily presented me with a toaster oven. There are a hundred moments in time, a hundred memories of her being her.

June standing in one of the well-appointed Casey House rooms, beaming down at my brother who lay wasting away, cracking jokes 'til he smiled. June was stopped every few feet on our way to dinner by men who had to tell her what she'd meant to their lives. And June, sending me that email, so typically her: "Eat your heart out, I've got cancer."

Laughter and light, that's what I'll remember, when things get hard, and the world closes in. Laughter and light.

Pat Capponi has lived the life that many are still trapped in; she has worked tirelessly and urgently to restore dignity and opportunity for those trapped in poverty, mental illness, and homelessness. She has written numerous works of non-fiction about poverty, mental illness, and policing as well as two mysteries set in a rooming house in Parkdale, Last Stop Sunnyside *and* The Corpse Will Keep.

Pat has served as a board member of CAMH, is a recipient of the Order of Ontario and the C.M. Hincks award from the Canadian Mental Health Association, and was a member of the Social Assistance Review Advisory Council. Currently, she is a part time member of the Consent and Capacity Board, and co-chairs the Toronto Police Services Board sub-committee on mental health. She is lead facilitator with Voices From the Street, a program that offers a twelve week course on leadership to the poor, homeless, those with mental health or addiction issues, and those with physical challenges, as well as newcomers. She has demonstrated the power of lived experience in leading this fight.

SHIRLEY DOUGLAS

WHEN KINDRED SPIRITS MEET everything is possible — even
the bleakest events in our lives are made more tolerable —
after we talk. Thank you for the pure joy of knowing you
— my shiny friend.

Shirley Douglas was born in Weyburn, Saskatchewan in 1934, grew
up there, then moved to Regina in 1944, when her father became
Premier of Saskatchewan. She started performing in the Regina
Little Theatre, the Banff School of Fine Arts, and then at the Royal
Academy of Fine Art in London, England. In 1953 she received her
equity card and, since then, has become respected for her acting
in films, on television, and on stage. She and her son, Kiefer, once
starred in The Glass Menagerie at the Royal Alexandra Theatre.

As an Officer of the Order of Canada, Shirley is also recognized
for her political advocacy — for the antiwar movement, for civil
rights and, in particular, for a universal healthcare system, which
is the legacy of her father, Tommy Douglas.

AFTERWORD ⌒

ON APRIL 2, 2007, in what was billed as her last interview — for the CBC's *The Hour with George Stroumboulopoulos* — June Callwood spoke in a relaxed fashion about her life, her accomplishments, and her love for Trent Frayne — her husband of sixty-three years — and for their family.

And then she spoke about her illness, with her usual direct and humorous approach. "I'm a mess," she said. "My cancer is all over the place. I'm blowing up like a Goodyear blimp, which I didn't think was supposed to happen. I thought you were supposed to get lean and beautiful."

George asked about what she might find in the hereafter. He received a prompt reply. "I reject the idea of heaven," she said. "There's nothing next. That's all right. What you get is a life. A baby is a miracle. You open a baby's fist and they'll close their hand on your hand and hold on. What they've got is a life to live as best as they can. That's what you get. You don't need anything else if you've got that."

She also rejected the idea of God. "I believe in kindness. I believe it's very communicable, just as meanness is. Strangers hold doors for one another. Sometimes they say thank you, sometimes they don't. Something in us says: 'If I hold this door it helps this person, then that person is slightly changed.' Great consideration for one another — that's what's going to save the world."

And she spoke of a new kind of physical intimacy that develops between a husband and wife as one spouse suffers from a terminal illness. They have become even closer, she said.

June said she had no regrets, except for not having more babies! She felt that her life had been full, with many accomplishments. "I'm a licensed pilot. I've flown an airplane. I swim in the ocean. I married the man I loved, had four wonderful kids — and I never did anything that I'm deeply ashamed of."

And after joking with George, telling him she had named a tumour after him, she admitted that she was ready to die. "I'm okay. I'm eighty-two years old for heaven's sake! Dust to dust is the way it ought to be. The death of the young is inexcusable." Then she smiled, turned to George, and said: "You're awfully good at your job!"

That was the June we knew and loved. After watching this final interview, I recalled something she had written years ago in her book *Emotions* (first published in 1964). In discussing the elderly, she wrote that "the tone for many is dark and grieving for lost mobility and shining face…. On the other hand, some old people seem purified of malice. They display benevolence, tolerance, sympathy, humour, appreciation. They give hope for the human race." June was, most certainly, in the latter group.

At one point during this memorable interview, June again said quietly: "I believe in kindness — and great consideration for others. That's what's going to save the world." And that is what we hope this book will help do.